Dramatic Monologues:
Making the Bible Live

# DRAMATIC
# MONOLOGUES

## RAYMOND BAILEY
## JAMES L. BLEVINS

**BROADMAN PRESS**
NASHVILLE, TENNESSEE

© Copyright 1990 ● Broadman Press
All rights reserved
4221-22
ISBN: 0-8054-2122-X
Dewey Decimal Classification: 815.008
Subject Heading: BIBLE - DRAMA // MONOLOGUES
Library of Congress Card Catalog Number: 89-48731
Printed in the United States of America

**Library of Congress Cataloging-in-Publication Data**
Bailey, Raymond, 1938-
  Dramatic Monologues : making the Bible live / Raymond Bailey.
  James L. Blevins.
  p. cm.
  ISBN: 0-8054-2122-X
  1. Monologue sermons. 2. Biographical preaching. 3. Baptists-
  -Sermons. 4. Sermons, American. 5. Bible--Biography--Sermons.
  I. Blevins, James L. II. Title.
  BV4307.M6B3 1990
  252' .061--dc20
                                                              89-48731
                                                                   CIP

# Contents

1. The Bible Is About People: Let Them Live ................ 7

2. Making Use of the Bible in Dramatic Monologues ........ 25

3. Moses: The Call from Contentment to Conflict ........... 43

4. Hosea: Love that Costs ................................. 51

5. Reflections of a New Mother .......................... 57

6. The Good Samaritan ................................... 63

7. Judas: The Plan that Failed ........................... 69

8. Peter: A Slow Learner ................................. 77

9. Encounter with Caiaphas .............................. 85

10. Pilate: Pragmatist .................................... 93

11. Encounter with Paul .................................. 99

12. Timothy: Journey to Ephesus ........................ 109

13. John: Rediscovering a Lost Book ..................... 117

Appendix: Resources ................................... 125

# 1

# The Bible Is About People: Let Them Live

The drama of redemption is an apt description of the literary content of the Bible. The Scriptures meet all the criteria for good dramatic literature. There is conflict, suspense, strong characters, and action. The sources of conflict are universal, making identification with people of all ages easy. Good drama is about life and that is certainly the subject of the Bible. Drama is most effective when it demands mental participation on the part of the reader or viewer.

Biblical drama is different in that it is revelation. God is revealed in His relationship to the world and His interaction with people. The readers or listeners discover themselves in the divine/human drama and learn about their possibilities for meaningful life. The Bible is the record of the revelation of God. He reveals to us Himself and ourselves. We are most gripped by a dramatic performance when we realize that what is happening on stage to the characters can happen, has happened, or will happen to us. Who would deny that the truth of Holy Scripture affects us most when we see that it is truth about us and for us? We do not interpret the Bible; it interprets us.

We should not be surprised that dramatic sermon forms are increasing in popularity and proving effective in having an impact on nonbelievers as well as believers. Persons who raise mental defenses at the mention of the word *sermon* and who are immediately hostile to the preacher's accusing finger and judgmental tone are vulnerable to the well-told story, the moving musical, the spectacular Easter pageant, the dialogue, or the dramatic first-person sermon. Dramatic techniques can be powerful means of overcoming natural resistance to persuasion as well as more common barriers such as boredom.

The Bible itself provides us with examples of such preaching devices. We would do well to view the Bible not only as the source of our authority but also as the best model of means of revelation. The Bible contains the world's greatest sermons and should be studied for effective communication models as well as for truth. For centuries, the story of Job has been retold in poetry and drama, sacred and profane. In the early days of American films, Cecil B. deMille made a career out of biblical spectacles. Biblical literature is story with a purpose, and its rhetorical intent would not stretch the category to describe much of the Bible as sermons. Preachers would do well to remember that the sermons most likely to evoke responses are those that in strong form communicate God's story which intersects with our stories.

### The Sermon as Drama

Story and drama work as sermons for a number of reasons. First, the inductive character of drama and story bypasses obstacles that deflect persuasive discourse. Contrast the approach of two preachers in dealing with cases of royal adultery. Nathan told David a story about the abuse of a poor man by a wealthy neighbor. It wasn't a story about sexual immorality, but it was a tale that demonstrated a commonly violated ethical principle. When the king heard such an obvious case of injustice, he was furious. He was led to make the judgment that would transform his life. When David realized that the story was about him, nothing was left except for him to repent. John the Baptist on the other hand used a more direct approach in attacking Herod and Herodias. John pointed an accusing finger and passed sentence. There was no subtlety in his approach. As a result of his choice of sermon form, John suffered the fate of many "bold," direct preachers and lost his head.

Jesus rarely preached in the style of the Greeks and Romans. Speeches were not His way. He did not philosophize or argue. He told stories that engulfed His listeners. As they listened to Him, people realized the stories were about them. Their identification with the characters and conflicts demanded self-examination and decision. People surely did not go home from an encounter with Jesus repeating cleverly alliterated points of a lecture or reconstructing arguments. They went home with a story, sometimes amusing, sometimes sad, but always a story about life that they could share with others. Jesus' stories presented more than abstract rules for clean living; they were models which could be acted out in the arenas of life. The stories of Jesus offered strategies for survival.

A second reason for the use of dramatic form is the power of symbolic action. The Passover meal, the Lord's Supper, and baptism provide examples of acts that communicate far more than formal discourses do. The story of Hosea and Gomer combines symbol and real life to form a powerfully acted parable that captures attention and speaks to intellect and feeling with equal force. People are more likely to respond and to sustain a response that appeals to both reason and emotion rather than a singular appeal to either.

Drama is also more likely to make a lasting impression than the mere transfer of information or logical argument. Truth in dramatic form is more memorable. Stories and actions are more easily recalled than propositions or even carefully paralleled points in a sermon. Most people do not hear the name of Simon of Cyrene without a mental image of a dark-skinned man bearing the cross for Christ. Mention of Peter, Paul, or Lydia will evoke a favorite story or scene, not a psychological analysis or theological dissertation. The scene of Pilate washing his hands is more vivid than any words he spoke at the trial. Christians speak of God's plan for the world and His church, and it is the plot, the unfolding biblical drama, that comes to mind. Christians brought up in Sunday School are more likely to remember the lessons of Eve and the serpent, Daniel in the lion's den, the Hebrew children in the furnace, the stilling of the storm, and so forth, than they are moralistic sermons. Principles of morality, kindness, and courage are remembered as demonstrations, not as memorized rules of conduct.

Drama, moreover, is an appropriate vehicle for Christian truth because it subordinates the messenger to the message. The preacher appropriately becomes a bridge between the source and subject. He or she is put in a position that encourages the sublimation of his or her personality to the personality of the writer or speaker. Preaching becomes an act of interpretation of persons or events rather than the promotion of self. Some personalities are so strong that they become an obstacle rather than a medium to God's message. The thoroughly prepared dramatic monologue sermon forces the preacher to become the voice of the biblical writer or the personality suggested by the biblical author. After I had presented a series of dramatic monologue sermons in a church I served, one of the children asked her mother why all the Bible people were heavy. She had not recognized the pastor who had held her in his arms, eaten with her on several occasions, and been frequently before her. She did have an image of a person with a biblical message.

Drama is a potent means of presenting the gospel because of its nature as action. The Greek word from which "drama" is derived means "a thing done." Drama suggests a truth in story form which is acted out. Paul interpreted preaching as an event, a happening. People are saved as a part of that event (1 Cor. 1:21). Paul spoke of proclamation as "demonstration of the Spirit and of power" (1 Cor. 2:4). While I do not contend that a dramatic form is the only form conducive to such an interpretation, I do believe it is a powerful one consistent with the message and method of Jesus and the dramatic prophets before Him.

One form of pulpit drama that can be used by every preacher in any setting or time is that of the first-person sermon. The first-person sermon is simply a form of role playing. The preacher strives to bring to life the thought and feeling of a biblical character. The preacher studies the Scriptures to try to determine why a person acted in a certain way or made a certain choice. Action is examined in the light of personality. Characters become models for contemporary choices. Sometimes they model bad behavior, sometimes good behavior. Modern congregations can identify with humans like themselves who make good and bad choices and live with the consequences.

Sermons usually have one of three purposes. They can be divided into the priestly, the prophetic, and the didactic. The priestly sermon has as its purpose the encouragement and support of those to whom it is addressed. The prophetic sermon indicts, judges, and challenges to action. The didactic presentation is designed to instruct. The collection of first-person sermons included in this book all fall into one of these three categories. Some of the sermons are more inspirational and remind the listener of God's providential care; some expose the consequences of bad choices and the perils of disobedience to God's will; others instruct in an interesting and memorable way. Some offer hope in diverse human crises, others warn of impending self-destruction, and still others instruct in the ways of abundant living. The point is that the dramatic monologue sermon can be used for any of these purposes.

### Preparation for the Dramatic Monologue Sermon

Dr. Blevins will deal with exegetical procedures and background studies in chapter 2; therefore, I will employ a literary approach to analyzing Scripture for the purpose of developing a dramatic monologue sermon. Attention will also be given to techniques for developing and delivering the sermon. It is assumed that a preacher respects, even reveres the Bible as uniquely inspired by God. The Bible merits special handling deserved by no other writing. Preparation for all sermons should begin with the prayerful solicitation of the leadership of the Holy Spirit. The Spirit who inspired the message and form of the original writer is available to inspire the contemporary interpreter how to best apply it to the people of this age and to a particular audience. One should not, however, discount the ability of the Holy Spirit to use the tools of literary analysis and good communication to reveal God's truth. The God of redemption is the God of creation and the Giver of all good and perfect gifts. Gifts of intellect, body, and feeling are to be used along with spiritual discernment.

Biblical characters are real persons or literary creations (as in the parables) endowed with human qualities. The human qualities, both strengths and weaknesses, must be identified in preparation for giving life to the character. The preacher should study carefully every passage in the Bible that in any way relates to the character in question. What do the Scriptures say about the person? What words does the person speak in Scripture? What do other characters say about the principal? What does church history and tradition contain about interpretation of the character?

Pilate presents an intriguing case study for consideration of biblical and nonbiblical sources. Each of the Gospels has its own perspective on Pilate. Pilate plays the role of an impartial judge in Mark. Matthew introduces Pilate's wife into the narrative and stresses the guilt of the Jews. Luke included more detail and added the judgment of Herod Antipas in support of Pilate's position. Luke stressed Pilate's declarations of Jesus' innocence and Pilate's attempts to set Him free. John's account differs from the Synoptic Gospels. In John, the philosophical question of truth is raised, and the mob participates more fully in the sequence of events. Pilate is assigned a more prominent role in the Johannine drama. He and Jesus are the central characters in the trial. John presented a Pilate struggling with his own sense of justice and political expediency. Jesus is portrayed as telling Pilate that the governor is not in control of events and is a helpless pawn. But the script gives the official several opportunities to act justly. Reliable extrabiblical historical sources do not tell us a great deal about Pilate. Only one passing mention of Pilate is found in Greco-Roman sources. Philo and Josephus portray the Roman official as cruel and inept. Postbiblical sources present conflicting opinions of Pilate. In some he is portrayed as a hero and a Christian convert; in others he is remembered as a coward who died a suicide. Pilate's wife's name does not appear in the Bible, but her name is given in literature of the early church where she is identified as Procula. Pilate and his wife are depicted as converts and saints in the Coptic tradition. In building a first-person sermon on Pilate, one may use part or all of these sources, but decisions must be made and should include nothing that conflicts with the biblical account. The Gospel chosen as the primary source should shape any characterization.

Various biblical persons assume great symbolic significance. David is a messianic figure. Job symbolizes suffering, Ruth is the model of loyalty, and Abraham is the prototype of the person of faith. The monologue may build on what the audience accepts about these persons, or it may play against popular perceptions. Most audiences, even nonchurch ones, will have preconceived ideas about the characters and their motives. The most stimulating sermons will be those that challenge traditional views often based *neither* on careful thought nor research.

Relationships are a key to understanding persons. Relationships reveal character and explain behavior. One cannot deal with Jacob without exploring the interaction with his mother Rebekah, father Isaac, and brother Esau. The story of Ruth depends somewhat on the relationship of Boaz to Elimelech. The relationships are rarely discussed or explained. In the Bible, as in life, behavior is the most reliable indicator of belief and values. David's strength of character is disclosed in his treatment of Saul, particularly in refusing to kill Saul when the opportunity presented itself (1 Sam. 24—26). David's vulnerability was demonstrated in his adultery with Bathsheba and the murder of Uriah (2 Sam. 11). It was not what the Hebrew children said, but what they did that made them heroes of faith. Human interventions reveal character and affect audience identification.

If the monologue is to focus on a single episode or passage, the scene or scenes must be carefully analyzed. Visualize the scene. Where does it take place? Who does what to whom? Who says what to whom? Are there statements or descriptions that suggest why those involved act as they do? Begin with the physical setting. Is the locale by the sea, in the mountains, in the city, or in a home? What is the climate, the time of day, and the season of the year? A sensory recreation will help you understand the passage as well as get the "feel" for your character. Imagine a picture of the scene. What do you see? The vegetation might be green with the sprinkled colors of flowers and various plants, or the place might be a barren desert setting. Look in your mind's eye at the shape of houses, boats, farms, and animals. Explore the sky and the distant horizon. Now you are ready to focus on people. How many are there? How old are they? Look at their physical shapes and into the faces of the crowd, if there is one, and, especially, look at the faces and bodies of the central figures in the story.

Next, let the picture move and imagine yourself a part of the action. What do you hear? Listen for the sounds of work and play, the everyday sounds of ordinary living. One of Jesus' special gifts was to make the ordinary extraordinary by experiencing it in a fresh way. The blowing of the wind, the whispering of the sea washing the shore, the hawking of wares in the streets, and customers bartering with merchants provided background music for the drama of Jesus. Odor has a greater influence on us than most of us realize. What were the smells of Jesus' world? Outdoor cooking, bodies without benefit of deodorants, sea smells, the smell of the sick and helpless who lived on street corners, the incense of the temple, the fragrance of the cedars, and the aroma of olives being pressed into oil.

Take accounts like that in John 5 by the pool of Bethesda and experience the sights, sounds, and smells of the scene. The Gospel of John tells us that there was a festival going on in Jerusalem. This means that the population may have been expanded to as much as three times the normal number of inhabitants. Movement would have been difficult. There would surely have been much noise and inconvenience, perhaps leading to short tempers. The major action took place in an area shunned by most travelers. It was occupied by a large number of sick people. Have you visited a busy emergency room lately? Have you ever visited a poorly operated convalescent home? There were no orderlies, doctors, nurses, painkillers, or antiseptics in the area near the sheep gate. Imagine the smell of the sheep path, of the unwashed bodies, open sores, and human waste. Hear the moans of the dying and the cries of pain. See the suffering of a "multitude of invalids, blind, lame, paralyzed" (5:4). The drama of Jesus' powerful acts of compassion is enhanced when one really has a "feel" for the scene.

Drama is built on action. Visualize the action of the scene. What did each participant in the scene feel? How did his or her dress affect action? The age and physical build of persons determines much of their movement. Persons' occupations will make a difference in their strength and movement; for example, a fisherman might have a stoop from bending and drawing nets filled with the catch. Women who carry huge jugs of water may have strong arms. Try to feel in your own body the effects of different occupations, climate, nutrition, and total life-style. Feel in your own body what it would be like to drag yourself to the pool or bend to minister to one of the helpless.

Analyzing the text should include a gauge of emotions as well as interpretation of meaning. Ask what emotions are contained in the narrative or in the combined narratives in which an individual is involved. What are the dominant emotions that explain words and acts? Is there love, anger, or fear? How can you explain the different emotions demonstrated by different characters? How would you react in a similar situation? In what circumstances have you experienced similar emotions? Recall how you felt. Did you have "butterflies" in the stomach? Were your muscles tense? Did you feel your heartbeat and pulse race? Did you feel hot and flushed or cold and clammy? As you are able to identify with the humanity of the people of the Bible, you are more able to learn from their experiences and to appropriate biblical truth for your own life. You are an important step closer to the practice of Christian truth. You are also closer to effective communication of biblical lessons to others. Sensory exploration is a good way to get inside a text in preparation for any kind of sermon. The sensitive explorer of Scripture has a sense of being there to bring the experience to the present.

## Plotting the Sermon

With the research out of the way, you are ready to move toward
writing the sermon script. There are some excellent ready-made
scripts in the Bible. Some of the best dramatic monologue sermons
are skillful oral interpretations of the text. Through the use of vocal
inflection, planned pauses, and pacing, you can communicate meaning to a congregation. What congregation would not profit from
hearing Paul with great feeling deliver the Letter to the Galatians?
Use a modern translation to address issues as real and important as
they were in the first century. Let Ruth tell her own story or Naomi
recount with loving humility God's provision for her and her daugh-
ter-in-law. Malachi might thunder God's judgment on indifferent
Christians just going through the motions of being religious. John's
First Epistle is an ideal sermon length and a message for every generation. Jude is about the right length for a prayer-meeting meditation.
The words will be right and the message on target when the scriptural
script is used. The preacher is free to focus on characterizations and
performance which will be discussed more fully below.

When you develop a sermon, the biblical text should still remain
primary. At this point read carefully the passage or passages from
which will emerge the sermon. If there are a number of passages,
combine them into a single narrative about the character. Next, para-
phrase. Write all you know about the person or event which will be
central to the sermon in a single story in your own words. Note that I
have said person or event. Sometimes the monologue sermon is about
an individual and teaches something about personal character and
action. You may, however, focus on an event and make the plot more
important than the character. The story of the healing of the blind
man in John 9 could be told from the viewpoint of the blind man, of
one of his parents, of one of the disciples, of one of the Pharisees, or
from the perspective of an anonymous observer. We really know
nothing of the personality, beliefs, or value system of the blind man.
Monologues are often done from the perspective of a beneficiary of a

miracle of Jesus. In these instances, the testimony reveals the before-and-after feelings of the healed person. How did the blind man feel about his affliction? Who, if anyone, did he blame? What was his social status, and how did he feel about Jesus after he was cured? What was this man's attitude toward the Pharisees who quizzed him about his healing? The intent of the Gospel writer was to give evidence of the power of Jesus and how different people reacted to it. From whatever viewpoint this story is told, the focus should be on Jesus. Whichever viewpoint is chosen, the monologue should reflect the intent of the text.

The narrative of the healing of the man by the pool of Bethesda recorded in John 5 and discussed above provides a good example of the many options one sometimes has in selecting a point of view. That particular story could be reported by the healed man, one of the disciples, a Pharisee, an unhealed victim of the disciples, an unhealed victim who lay nearby, or a passing observer. A report by an uninvolved observer often provides the greatest freedom to the interpreter. When this is done, there is no need to provide any psychological insight into the spokesperson and no religious history is really necessary. The speaker is merely an interpretative reporter describing and interpreting the events and the reaction of those present. This technique allows a male preacher to deal with female characters. One of the disciples could describe and explain his reaction to Jesus' encounter with the woman at the well recorded in John 4. A Pharisee might criticize Jesus for His association with various women. Paul could recall Priscilla or Lydia. Timothy might speak of the women in his life. Of course, a woman could reverse the process with male characters and offer a female perspective. This kind of sermon focuses on plot, that is, on the action and therefore requires more action than a character profile sermon.

The dramatic monologue sermon plot has the same requirements of any good sermon. There should be suspense, action, and interesting people. You might ask how the dramatist can create suspense when the ordinary church congregation has heard the biblical stories over and over. Of course, the traditional sermon has to overcome the same problem. Here we can learn from secular literature. Some of the world's greatest drama was written by the Greek playwrights who created their dramas from the material of familiar myths. From childhood, the people knew the folklore and the outcome of each tale. What the playwrights did was fill in the blanks and reveal motives and internal conflicts. Characters were followed through the decision process and life events that may have affected choices. Alternative actions and possible consequences as well as motives were explored. Preachers handle material in a similar fashion every Sunday. The preacher draws out background exposition about how the persons involved in a story come to the point of crisis. He stresses the alternatives and relates the issues to contemporary life. Listeners are told their alternatives and the potential consequences of their choices. The Bible tells us that Peter had a mother-in-law (Matt. 8:14; Mark 1:30; and Luke 4:38), but no mention is made of a wife in the Gospels. First Corinthians 9:5, however, indicates that in the postresurrection period Peter had a wife who traveled with him. Was he widowed in the earlier period and later remarried? Was there other family? How was his life affected by his family relationship? One might also comment on Peter's relationship with his mother-in-law. If one chooses to believe that Peter's wife was living while he traveled with Jesus, there is still an angle to be developed. Why is she never mentioned? In either case, how did Peter's marriage and his wife's life affect his life? One can only speculate about the family Abraham left behind, the background of many of the prophets, or what was in Judas's background that made him betray Jesus. We learn in Joshua 24 that Abraham's family worshiped other gods. How did that influence Abraham's response to God's call? What was Abraham's relationship to his family after he left home to answer God's call?

Does not every preacher at some time attribute motives for various actions where they are not stated in Scripture? Why did Moses turn aside to examine the burning bush (Ex. 3:3)? What would have happened if he hadn't? The Lord spoke to Moses only after he turned aside: "When the Lord saw that he turned aside to look, God called to him" (Ex. 3:4, NASB). What went through the rich young ruler's mind when he chose his possessions over eternal life? Why didn't Nicodemus become a public disciple of Jesus before the Lord's trial and crucifixion? Was Bartimaeus blind from birth (Mark 10:46)? How did he become a beggar? What was his relationship to his family? Here is an opportunity to teach a congregation a great deal about Jewish society in the first century. What happened to Bartimaeus after he was healed?

The Bible invites sermonizing by succinctness and by the openness of the stories. Unlike other ancient literature such as Homer's writings, scriptural accounts are for the most part plot outlines with sparse details. Preaching space is open in the nature of biblical narrative. What happened to the elder brother in the parable (Luke 15:11-32), and what were the consequences of the rich young ruler's choice (Luke 18:18-23; Matt. 19:16-29; and Mark 10:17-30)? One conservative pastor preached a Mother's Day sermon on the mother in the parable of the prodigal son. His entire sermon reflected on her feelings and actions although the text says nothing about her. I am reluctant to go that far inasmuch as there is no hint of a mother in the parable, but this demonstrates how exploring between the lines is not uncommon in the pulpit.

Every sermon, including the monologue, should have a beginning, a middle, and an end. A setting with alternatives must be established. There must be real choices to be made. If the interest of the audience is to be maintained, there must be genuine conflict with internal or external forces or both. The rich young ruler struggled with his own values, his fears, and the false security of his possessions. He was a first-century yuppie. Pilate had to deal with his Roman values, his Roman superiors, the mob, the Jewish leaders, and his wife. He was a practical politician like many today. Gideon's enemies were the Midianites as well as his low self-esteem. Samson had Delilah with whom to deal, and Elijah had Ahab. The skillful preacher will find ways to make these opposing forces sound contemporary so the audience can identify with the struggle as well as the person.

Each sermon needs a climax, a high point, and the moment of truth. The climax may be physical, emotional, or intellectual. Monologues will nearly always have an emotional or intellectual climax although a physical one may be depicted or implied. The conclusion of the Judas sermon, included in this collection, has Judas running screaming into the night, apparently to hang himself. The best climaxes will demand an emotional and intellectual response from the congregation. The people will be led to a decision with or against the character.

The "end" of the piece must answer the "So what?" question. A sermon should always have a specific purpose. As a result of encountering a biblical truth, some specific response should be expected from the congregation. This is usually accomplished in the monologue sermon by making clear the consequences of certain choices, the joy or sorrow that has resulted from the character's pilgrimage, or the conclusions based on the recreation of an event. You must be cautious at this point not to break character and become "preachy." The special effectiveness of the dramatic sermon lies in its subtle inductive nature. Direct appeal to the congregation is rarely effective: it breaks the mood and the sense of "being there." Any invitation by the character should be a universal and general one. In the sermons in this collection, Peter is the only one to give a direct challenge. Most of the time, the invitation should be issued by someone other than the preacher. Whoever gives the invitation should base the appeal on the message. The one giving the invitation should not, however, "explain" the monologue. The invitation should be clear from the sermon.

Characterization is always important and usually dominant in dramatic monologue sermons. The characters should be multidimensional and believable. The temptation is to make biblical personalities all good or all evil. The principal figures in the Bible are portrayed as fully human with all the frailty of corrupt humanity. God has opted to disclose His heroes and heroines with all their warts. Peter in one moment made the greatest confession in history and in the next incurred Jesus' rebuke (Matt. 16:16,23). Abraham, David, Joseph, Peter, and Paul—these all made mistakes. It is for this reason that sinners, saved by grace, can identify with them. Thoughts, speech, and actions should reveal these biblical characters as persons who struggled to understand, sometimes misunderstood, who laughed and cried, hungered and hurt. They were not always noble, and at times they made foolish mistakes. They used "holy" language less than most contemporary preachers. Sometimes they shouted, and sometimes they mumbled. If they are to have the desired effect in the pulpit, they must be believable. There are some queens, kings, and other persons of noble birth and position in the Scriptures, but most of the people who come alive in Scripture are simple people with the hopes and fears of common folks. Even some of the kings were of rather common origin. They were people like us who became special because they were a part of God's plan. Because they are like us, we should understand and be able to portray them.

The preacher strives to bring the universal truth of Scripture across the ages in a way that each generation can understand and appropriate it. There are four approaches to overcoming the distance of time and culture. The most obvious is to transport a contemporary congregation back to an ancient time. This approach requires the preacher to be as authentic as possible in costume, makeup, language, metaphor, and thought forms. A second approach is to bring the past into the present by using contemporary idioms and modern dress. The elder brother might be presented as a modern yuppie businessman whose brother has lost it all in New York or Los Angeles. One might choose to use modern dress but keep the script pure by using ancient idioms and cultural references. The fourth possibility would be: use costume and makeup to suggest the original setting but employ modern language and contemporary cultural references and metaphors. It is imperative that a writer make a decision about which style is to be used in a particular sermon script and then be consistent throughout the whole piece. A common error is slipping New Testament language and ideas into the minds and mouths of Old Testament characters.

Modern theological terms should not be imposed on characters no matter which style is chosen. It would be poor exegesis and dishonest preaching to put a word like *rapture* on the lips of an Old Testament or Gospel character. The word and concept is unknown in those contexts, and it would mislead contemporary listeners. One should not expect the Old Testament prophets to speak of "church" or "baptism."

## Presenting the Sermon

Concentration and control are the keys to effective delivery of the dramatic sermon. You must become the character and seek to think each line and feel each emotion as the character. In your mind's eye, you must see the original scene, people, and events that were a part of God's unfolding revelation. Look at the world as Lydia, Priscilla, Phoebe, Elijah, Samson, Peter, and Paul saw it. Don't just speak memorized words, share thoughts, and communicate truth as the character has experienced it. Limit your knowledge in the role to the knowledge that the biblical character had at the time he or she is speaking. You are seeking to reproduce thoughts and emotions from another time and place. Sustain belief in who you are portraying. You can be convincing only if you have sought to understand how the characters thought and why they acted as they did. Don't make Mary a modern older adolescent because her tender age (probably twelve or thirteen) at the birth of Jesus offends. Don't impose modern morals on ancient characters.

Don't attempt a character for which you cannot develop some empathy. Play the character, don't judge or mock the person. To portray Ahab, Jezebel, Judas, or Simon Magnus, you must try to understand the nature of their evil, the motivation of their evil deeds, and you must believe that under similar circumstances you might have made the same sinful choices.

Control of mind, body, and voice is essential. All must work together. The words, physical movements, and vocal inflections must all convey the same message. Emotions must be felt from the bottom of your feet to the top of your head. Large gestures and grand movements will look out of place on most church platforms. Gestures should appear as natural expressions of feeling rather than staged motions for emphasis. Clear, simple movements will be most successful. Every gesture and movement should have a purpose and be coordinated with thought and emotion. A facial scowl and harsh tone are not credible from a relaxed body. Words that express anger are unconvincing delivered by a soft, pleasant voice.

The primary instrument of the preacher is the voice. Pitch and rate can help to establish a character's age as well as emotional level. A lower pitch and slower rate suggest an older person. Social status is often reflected in distinctive articulation, proper pronunciation, and enunciation. Colloquial expressions and slang are characteristic of the uneducated and lower social classes. An unfamiliar accent will create a sense of distance. The use of certain British pronunciations or a general light British accent for a character like Pilate will suggest aristocracy. The intentional use of incorrect grammar for people like the shepherds can establish their lowly place in Jewish society. Extreme affectation is to be avoided. Each speaker must appear comfortable and natural in his or her expression. A principle worth remembering is that any technique that draws too much attention to itself and away from the content and purpose of the sermon should be avoided. If people leave talking about your voice, makeup, or whatever rather than the message, you have failed.

Characterization aside, certain principles of good oral communication should be followed. Rhythm should not be left to chance. Rhythm expresses intensity and provides variety. All of us have certain rhythmic speech patterns. This would be true of every person portrayed. Listen to different people of various ages, educational, and cultural levels and note their speech patterns. In playing characters who are like them, remember and imitate those patterns. Use variety and contrast in rhythm for emphasis.

Conscious use should be made of the dramatic pause. Pauses for effect should be planned. Pauses are important to all kinds of public speaking. If there are too many or too long, they will bore the listeners. In the right proportion, pauses allow the listener to assimilate, analyze, and draw a desired conclusion. Work for the pregnant pause, one that is filled with meaning waiting to be born. Pitch ought to be varied according to the normal pitch of a person under a given emotion. Gradual increases and decreases will build to the planned climax and then the resolution. Sudden changes express intense feeling. Volume is also a means of emphasis and variety. Beginners often overuse loudness as a means of emphasis. A stage whisper or lowered volume is often tremendously effective. The key is contrast. Dramatic effect aside, the speaker must speak loud enough and clear enough to be understood by everyone present.

Every sermon should be rehearsed. Rehearsal is essential for the dramatic monologue sermon. The preacher would be wise to spend some time with a tape recorder and some time in front of a mirror. If an amplification system is to be used, the preacher should practice with it to adjust volume and pitch, and so forth. Some practice should take place on the platform with the physical arrangements as they will be in the worship service. If a costume is going to be used, it should be worn during practice to assure freedom of movement and to lessen self-consciousness.

The dramatic monologue sermon requires research and much preparation. The result, however, is worth the effort. This sermon form is an effective way to communicate the gospel.

# 2
# Making Use of the Bible in Dramatic Monologues

The primary focus of biblical dramatic monologues is to make the characters real and alive. Sometimes you can overdo that a bit. Recently, I was invited to role play John, the writer of Revelation, at a large downtown church. The eleven o'clock worship service was on television. I was to enter the sanctuary at exactly 11:30 AM in time for the sermon. I came to the sanctuary door at 11:25 AM in my costume as John. My hair was long and gray, and my robes were a bit tattered from my prison experience. Much to my surprise, the usher at the door would not let me into the sanctuary. I knew the TV camera would be focused on the door at exactly 11:30. What would happen if no one entered through it? I had to do a lot of talking to convince the usher to let me in the sanctuary. He thought that I was a street person!

This same church was without a pastor at that time. Following the worship service, I received a phone call. A lady on the line exclaimed, "I really did enjoy your sermon today, but why did the church call such an old pastor?" The person doing the role play should strive to make it real. There is nothing worse than encountering a biblical character who seems false or artificial. Even worse is meeting a personality of the Bible who is uncertain of the biographical facts of the role. Before you venture forth to do a dramatic monologue, you should plan to spend some time with the character you propose to present. That involves Bible study. How does one approach the Bible for this purpose?

### Know How to Study the Bible

Before doing a dramatic monologue, one must learn how to study the Bible. One must come to the Bible in a stance of faith. The Bible is full of men and women of faith. These are the people you will want to meet and later portray. You must sense their faith. In John 20:31 we read, "These are written that you may believe." In faith, the Bible is designed to bring individuals to faith in Jesus Christ. The sole purpose is to bring about a yes to what God has done in our Lord. One cannot come to the Word of God in a detached mood. One cannot read it without some personal bias that in this case would be a faith commitment. The Bible takes on authority for those who believe in the God that is revealed in the Bible. Thus, the Bible cannot really be studied as just any other book. Often it is studied in the university classroom as fine literature, but it is more than that.

Many people when they first visit the Holy Land are greatly disappointed with the Jordan River. They expected a river the size of the Mississippi or the Ohio. In reality, it seems just a small muddy stream. Yet for the Jews it is liquid history. Much history has transpired on its banks. If one is really to appreciate the Jordan, one must enter in to that long history. No outsider can ever be caught up by the meaning of the Jordan as are the Jews. Likewise, no one outside the faith can really ever encounter the Bible as someone within the faith. Here the work of the Holy Spirit is vitally important. According to 2 Timothy 3:16, the Holy Spirit inspired the Scriptures, and the Spirit must quicken those who read the Scriptures to bring about a response of faith and also guide into all truth (John 16:13). In the Bible one must read with the heart open to the Spirit of God to receive from Him the gift of faith.[1]

One must come to Bible study with an open mind and an open heart to the revelation of God. In recreating a biblical character, one must be sensitive to the Spirit moving within and respond to God in words and in thoughts. The Bible must also be studied in the fellowship of the church. The biblical books were chosen on the basis of the help that they afforded early congregations. You might study the Bible alone, but you would miss the rich rewards that come through group Bible study. The community was a strong force in the Old Testament days as well as in the New Testament days. Personal Bible study should be accompanied by group study. Test out your ideas about a biblical character with a Sunday School class.

If you intend to do a dramatic monologue, you have a grave responsibility as a biblical teacher. One of the great roles of the church has always been that of teaching. Even the role of pastor is strongly related to the responsibilities of teaching. Throughout the New Testament we find words such as *preaching* and *teaching* in reference to the pastor. It is within the community of believers that we encounter good teachers who lead us into the depths of the Word of God. So often house groups study the Bible without a teacher; such groups can end up in being shared ignorance. Within the fellowship, teachers who have been trained and led of the Spirit can lead into the depth of the Word of God. In the communion of saints, we enlarge, supplement, and deepen a correct personal Bible study. This kind of encounter with Scripture can be done very well through a dramatic monologue.

The Bible must also be studied with open ears. Within the Word of God, there are injunctions to change one's life-style. Radical obedience is also necessary in response to the study of the Word of God. As you research your biblical character, your life might be changed! Often in the New Testament, Jesus would say to those who sought to follow Him, "Foxes have holes, and the birds of the air have nests, but the Son of Man has nowhere to lay His head" (Luke 9:58, NASB). Other times He would say, "Leave the dead to bury their own dead" (Luke 9:60). He called for a radical commitment. The Word of God still has that kind of power today.

Many great movements in Christianity have been started by reading the Word of God. Martin Luther, a Roman Catholic monk, devoted months of study to the Book of Romans. As he read and studied the book, Luther became convinced by the Spirit of the weakness of his own personal faith. So much of his religious experience had been based upon works. His study brought him to the need to reform the faith that he had. Luther wanted to bring about a spiritual revolution within the church. Unfortunately, the church was not ready for that and expelled him, helping to forge the Protestant Reformation. In portraying Paul, you, too, might be overwhelmed anew by the message of Romans.

### Methods for Bible Study

Now let us look at some methods for studying the Bible. In constructing a biblical character, it is very important when we come to the Bible not to select one passage out of context. Someone has said: the Bible is a fiddle on which one can play any tune. This is often true with a proof-text method of Bible study in which you read through the Bible and select one verse to support some argument or program that you are endeavoring to set forth. First of all, you must grasp the basic salvation message of the whole Bible. A basic formula for good Bible interpretation would be set in terms of mathematical formula. The biblical message over the biblical world equals the biblical message over the modern world.[2] It is very important in Bible study to go back and see what the biblical message meant in the day and time in which it was written. Here it is very important to read the history of the period, either Old Testament or New Testament, to discover the way people lived, walked, dressed, and what they ate. If at all possible, go back and put yourself into the shoes of the people who were living then. Hear the Word of God as your biblical character would have heard it.

The world has changed radically in two or three thousand years since our Bible was written. Words have new meanings. Customs have changed. An injunction given in one setting may be very different from an injunction given today. Then take that same eternal biblical message and put it over the modern world. What is the message within the context of our own culture today? In many Sunday School classes or in private Bible studies, one side of this formula is stressed over the other side. Sometimes we make Bible study all dead history. We spend the complete hour or two hours understanding what the biblical days were like. In other Bible studies, we only hear what the message means in our own world. We cut off the message from its roots in the past. We see this type of exegesis often in the Book of Revelation where, in many interpretations, it would seem that Revelation had no meaning in the day and time in which it was written. We hear only of modern nations such as Russia and the United States and what role they are going to play in the end event, not realizing that 2000 years ago such nations were not in existence and would have had no meaning for people living then.

Good sound biblical interpretation will include both sides of the formula. Then one must take the individual book being studied and try to learn more about the one who wrote the book. God allowed human beings to write down His Word, thus there is both the human and the divine element within our Bible. Each writer was allowed to express his own words. Mark's words, Mark's style, and Mark's vocabulary are quite different from that of Paul or John. Make sure you notice these traits if you are portraying one of these personalities. In our New Testament there are twenty-seven unique books. Redaction criticism is a tool by which we can study the individual writers and what each contributed to the Word as they wrote it down and shared it with others. We need to discover what individual qualities of writing can be found for each of our authors. We should attempt to discover what we can learn about the writer's life and background. This makes Bible study much more interesting.

Then look at the book as a whole. How does the biblical character in question fit into the whole book? It is rather unfortunate that chapter and verse divisions were put into our Bibles. Somehow in Bible study we miss the whole book; in Sunday School, we study two or three verses this Sunday, five or six verses the next Sunday. Many people never really encounter the book as a whole. Look for its literary patterns, its stylistic effects. Try to discover the basic purpose for each book as you read it. Then measure the book that you are studying against other books within the New Testament or Old Testament. Also try to discover who were the first readers of the book. What were their basic concerns?

For example, if you were dealing with John, a character from Revelation, it would be important to understand that the book was written in a period of persecution: A.D. 95. A new Caesar had come to power named Domitian. He believed he was divine, set up statues of himself all over the Roman Empire, and asked people to fall down and worship his statue three times a day. If you did not do this, you could not buy food in the marketplace. Those who did were tattooed on the backs of their hands or on their foreheads. This was the only way they could buy food. Revelation makes so much more sense if one puts it against that background. John was in prison writing to Christians who were also being persecuted and suffering death. Other tragedies had also broken out within the church. In this prison kind of setting, John received a message to the churches.

He was led to write Revelation in the symbolical coded language of the Jewish people. The coded language was called the Apocalyptic Code and involved numbers, colors, and animals. To understand the Book of Revelation, one must also understand these codes. It is a different kind of literature. Numerous books were written 200 years before Christ in this same code. Jewish people have been a persecuted people, and to share their faith they had to use codes. When one takes the time to do this kind of background study, then a biblical book that is often said to be difficult to understand becomes much more understandable. You might portray John on Patmos and let him give a historical introduction to his book.

A good way to find this kind of information—date, authorship, and readers—is to go to a good introduction to the Old Testament or to the New Testament. Two good sources are *The Interpreter's Bible* or *The Broadman Bible Commentary.* You should also consult a Bible dictionary. A very good Bible dictionary is the *Interpreter's Dictionary of the Bible* in four volumes, plus a supplementary volume to update it. Within this four-volume set are numerous articles by the best scholars in the United States. Almost every subject, name, and geographical place in the Bible—a world of information—is found therein. It is also very important to have a good series of commentaries on the biblical books. We have mentioned two. Yet, within the biblical field there are great classical commentaries. If you are just beginning Bible study, do not buy a series of commentaries but select the best book written on each of the biblical books. For example, on the Gospel of Mark, Vincent Taylor's fine commentary[3] is the great authority. On the Book of Revelation, George Caird[4] has an excellent commentary. One could go through all sixty-six books of the Bible and find the leading scholars on each of the books. Commentaries are very useful for difficult passages. Perhaps the biblical material for your character contains one or two difficult passages to understand. Almost every biblical book that you study or read has one or two difficult passages. It is very necessary to look and see what interpreters have had to say over the years on these passages.

Another help can be found in word studies. A very helpful series in the New Testament is edited by Kittel and called *The Theological Dictionary of the New Testament.*[5] You can look up any major word in the New Testament and find an article written on this word. The only drawback is that you must look up the word in the Greek, but, of course, the articles are written in English. These word studies are also available for the Old Testament.

The Bible can never be fully explored. Men and women have devoted their lives to Bible study and have never really reached the point where they can say they are satisfied with what they have accomplished. The Bible is the kind of Book that can be studied and restudied. It is like an endless well of water. Persons encounter new meanings, new understandings, which they have never seen before. Bible study is an exciting kind of challenge. You will never explore fully your biblical personality. The Bible is a book which covers hundreds of years of history but yet has a consistency of purpose and theme. It contains many different writers with their own unique styles that make it a very interesting Book to read. Many of the books in the Bible are fine literary examples, but they are more than that. They teach and bring forth faith in human hearts.

Let us now take our example book again, the Book of Revelation, since it is such a difficult text and filled with problems. Perhaps for your dramatic monologue from the Book of Revelation, you would want to go back and read about the period of time in which the book was written. It would be helpful then to go to a good Bible commentary, find the volume on the Book of Revelation, and read the introductory sessions about it. Learn something about the people who lived in the seven cities with their seven churches. Discover the cities as real cities in the ancient world. A very helpful tool at this point would be the *Biblical Illustrator* that the Southern Baptist Sunday School Board publishes. This periodical often has special features on the cities of the Old Testament and New Testament periods. Recently, there was a series on the seven cities of the Book of Revelation. You might want to introduce the city by playing the role of mayor of that city. Read such articles and discover the people in that day and time.

One should also learn something about persecution and suffering of the churches in the first centuries. The *Interpreter's Bible* will help you find all of that. Learn more about John's imprisonment and much more about the special kind of literature that Revelation is: apocalyptic and coded literature. Study or read other such books like the Book of Enoch.

When you can appreciate Revelation and its historical significance, start a chapter-by-chapter study of the book using a good commentary. Read the biblical passage in several different translations, underline difficult or hard passages in which to interpret, and look these up in a commentary. Single out place names or words that are difficult and look them up in a good Bible dictionary. Once you have discovered the biblical meaning in its own time, ask questions such as: What does this mean in my day and time? Do not be so overly concerned about the future in the Book of Revelation. Revelation has all three tenses; past, present, and future. It is very important to discover the past and the present, then you will see also implications for the future. Using these methods with the help of the Spirit and with the prayer of faith you can come to a better understanding of any biblical book, including Revelation. The character you chose to portray from Revelation will then be real and alive for your audience.

## Know the Central Biblical Message

If you are going to dramatize a biblical character, you must view that character against the central message of the Old and New Testament. A history of salvation runs throughout both the Old and New Testaments. The character you portray should never be seen in isolation. He or she is a part of God's greater plan or design.

The most helpful design that we could select for the salvation story in both Old and New Testaments would be the basic hourglass figure.[6] Can you imagine what an hourglass looks like? Broad at the top, very narrow at the middle, then it broadens again at the bottom. The sand trickles slowly from the upper sphere down to the lower sphere. Compare the biblical revelation to this hourglass diagram. At the top we see its broadest point: creation. God created all humankind. Then from the descendants of Adam and Eve, God selected a people to be His own.

Thus, the hourglass continues to narrow as we come to Abraham and Israel. Yet even in Israel, not all Jews were true Jews and followers of God. It was necessary for God to select a remnant, those who were faithful to Him down through world history. Then from the remnant we reach the narrow part of the hourglass—the appearance of the long-awaited One: Jesus Christ, the Son of God. Following that, the hourglass begins to broaden once again. As Jesus selected twelve disciples, these disciples taught and established His church. In Acts, the church continued to expand from 120 to thousands as the Word of God was proclaimed. The hourglass continues to broaden as the church receives its mission to proclaim the Word of God to all humankind. Then we look forward to the ultimate goal: a new creation in which all will sing the praise of God.

You will notice connections between groups on the hourglass figure. There is a connecting line on the top of the hourglass to the bottom: the old creation and the new creation, Adam and Eve connected to humankind, Abraham and Israel with the line of connection to the church, and the remnant with the line connected to the apostles. In the middle stands the Lord Jesus Christ. Every biblical character stands at some point in God's divine plan or design.

### Know the Biblical Languages

What translation shall I use? The success of dramatic monologues depends upon the flow of the language. First, you must realize the basic truth that every translation of the Bible is an interpretation. When we come to the biblical text, we are dealing with two foreign languages. The Old Testament was written in Hebrew, and the New Testament was written in Greek. Thus, the interpreter of the Bible has to deal with all the problems involved in bringing one language or two languages into modern English. Thousands of years have gone by since the first writing of some of the passages in our Bible. The character which you have chosen to dramatize may have lived thousands of years ago. Customs and attitudes have changed over the years. Interpreters of the Bible must deal with this vast problem of translation of the Bible into English.

If you are doing an Old Testament character, then you must first realize that your person spoke Hebrew. The Hebrew language is very difficult. From our perspective, it is written backwards. Writing goes from right to left on the page. The Hebrew reader began at the back of the book and read forward. Also in its earliest stages, Hebrew did not use vowel sounds. It was a language of consonants. Words were easily confused because of the lack of vowels. A famous example has to do with the statue of Moses by Michelangelo. Those who view the statue in Rome, see a great big horn on its head. The Latin Vulgate translation which Michelangelo was using had misinterpreted the Hebrew word for "halo" or bright light. The Bible tells us that Moses came down from Mount Sinai, his head surrounded by a bright light.

The words *horn* and *halo* are so very close in Hebrew the Latin Vulgate translated the text that Moses came down with his face "horned." An error in interpretation was etched into stone by Michelangelo. Thus, the Bible translator has to deal with a very complicated language which in many ways is very primitive. One must take forms and expressions of that language and translate them into modern English.

If you are dramatizing a New Testament personality, then you must realize that he or she spoke the Greek language. Greek was a very cultivated and developed language. For example, there are two different words for life in Greek. *Zoe* means life in the sense of quality living and *bios* symbolizes that which goes into making up life: food, shelter, and clothing. Our English translations translate both words as *life.* The prodigal son asked his father to divide his "life" (*bios*) with him. In other words, the son wanted the materialistic aspects of life. When the prodigal returned, the father made the statement that he was dead, but now he is alive (*zoe*).

We miss subtleties of expression in English. For example in Greek, there are three different words for love: *agape*, self-sacrificing love; *philos*, brotherly love; and *eros*, sexual love. In our English translations, little attempt is made to distinguish between the words. All are translated "love." Hence we must remember in translation, there is no exact equivalent for one word in one language and another word in another language. When I was studying in Germany, I was asked to go out and preach a sermon in German. I was preaching on the text of Jesus feeding the five thousand. I was nervous about preaching in a foreign language and proceeded to read my text, delivered my sermon, and even told a few American jokes. Nobody laughed. Finally when I came to the main point of my sermon, I said, "Jesus fed the five thousand people." Everyone broke out into laughter. I really did not know what I had said until the end of the sermon. An old lady came forward and asked me if I knew what I had said in my sermon. I said, "No, why did everybody laugh?" She said, "At the most intense part of your sermon, you said in German, 'And Jesus ate the five thousand people.'" The German words "to eat" and "to feed" are very similar, and I had mixed them up.

An amusing story was told by missionaries who first preached to the Eskimo people. Soon they had long lines of people outside their quarters wanting to go to hell because it was such a hot and warm place. Later, the missionaries had to depict hell as a cold forbidding, icy place to get across the same idea. In some Bibles translated into African dialects, Jesus is called the giraffe of God because in many parts of Africa there are no sheep or lambs. Every translator then is attempting to take a thought pattern in one language and place it into that of another language. There are multitudes of translations.

Select a translation for your biblical character that is accurate but yet flows! A guide for grading the major translations can be helpful at this point. In the *A* group of translations we would put those that have been brought forth by groups of people. Anytime a number of scholars get together comparing notes, debating and critiquing one another's translations, the translation is more likely to be accurate. The *King James Version* was translated by a group of scholars in England that the king had called together. The *Revised Standard Version* was brought forth by the best group of American scholars. The *Good News Bible* in part was brought about by a group of scholars as well as the *New International Version.*

The *B* group of translations would be those brought about by one individual. You can see right away that this would have its obvious weaknesses. An individual translating would not have the aid of contemporaries or colleagues to critique the work. Such one-person translations would be those of Williams and Goodspeed. *C* group translations are brought forth by church groups. The danger in these translations is that the church translation might be influenced or tipped in favor of supporting certain doctrines in that church. Some of the more famous church translations are the *New World Translation* by Jehovah's Witnesses and the *Douay Version* by the Roman Catholic Church. However, if you use a church translation, you should compare it with other translations to detect the differences. The fourth group would be *D* grade. These are interpolations or paraphrased translations. The writer makes no attempt to give a word-for-word translation and freely interprets the Scripture for you. The danger is that many Christians read the paraphrased translations and view them as word-for-word translations. Many of these translations also might be tipped in favor of a specific school of interpretation of theology. *The Living Bible* is a good example of this type of paraphrased translation.

Read through the Scripture passage for your character in each of the four kinds of translations. Select the one that expresses the character's personality the best.

### Know the Land of the Bible

To know your biblical characters, you must know something about the land in which they lived. Many people when they think of the Holy Land imagine a land of immense size with rivers the size of the Mississippi or the Ohio. Actually, Palestine is a very small country, smaller than many of our fifty states. In fact, in many of the states in which we live, Palestine would be the size of a few large counties, from north to south barely 200 miles, from east to west, seventy-five miles at its greatest extent.

Yet throughout history, this tiny postage-stamp land has wielded a great amount of political power. The reason Palestine has been in such a strategic location is: the country is located on the land ridge between Asia and Africa. All the mighty battle forces of world history have passed through this tiny land, and, in many cases, some of the great battles shaping world history have been fought there. In many ways, Palestine has been the battlefield for that part of the world.

Starting in the far north at Mount Hermon, the largest mountain in Palestine towering over 9,000 feet, the Jordan River begins. The river begins its journey southward, entering into the Sea of Galilee on the north shore, leaving the Sea of Galilee on the southern shore. The Sea of Galilee is the largest fresh-water body in Palestine. It is some twelve miles long and five miles across. It is located in a depression

696 feet below sea level. It is one of the most beautiful places in Palestine. Lovely, wild flowers grow around its banks. The climate is perfect for growing fig and fruit trees.

The temperature there stays very pleasant all winter, much like our Florida. It can be a very hot area, 110 degrees, in the summertime. The lake is in a depression, as we have said, and it is ringed by high mountains. The hot sun beats down on the lake in the summertime, but occasionally the winds will shift, and the only opening in the ring of mountains is to the north. The cold winds blowing off snow-covered Mount Hermon will hit the hot lake and cause very violent and sudden storms. We encounter these storms as we read the four Gospels. Quite often, Jesus and the disciples were caught in such storms as they traveled back and forth across the Sea of Galilee. In Jesus' day and time, there were many villages around the lake. The area was much more inhabited than it is today. Small villages of one to two thousand people encircled the lake. The sea was filled with fish, and many people made their living by fishing. All fishing was done in the evening because of the heat of the day. If you do a biblical character from Galilee, make the geography behind the person come alive.

The Jordan River leaves the Sea of Galilee and starts its trip down towards the Dead Sea. The River is very erratic in its course and flows very quickly, for we are moving even further below sea level. The Sea of Galilee, as we said, is 696 feet below sea level, but the Dead Sea is 1,290 feet below sea level, the lowest place on the face of the earth. The trip then from the Sea of Galilee to the Dead Sea provides us with a very quick river full of rapids. The area along the Jordan River is very fertile. Today it serves as the border of Israel and the nation of Jordan.

Our last major body of water is the Dead Sea, one of the most impressive seas on earth. The whole Jordan River Valley leading to the Dead Sea is part of a great rift valley running through the Middle East and down into Africa. The Dead Sea is called by that name because it is a salt sea. The waters of the sea are five times saltier than our oceans, the Atlantic and Pacific. In fact, it is very difficult to drown in the Dead Sea. The Romans, after they took Jerusalem in A.D. 70, took some of the Jewish leaders down to the Dead Sea to drown them. The Jews were subjected to the horror of drowning attempts all afternoon. No life can survive around the Dead Sea. There is no outlet to the sea as we see in our picture, so all the water evaporates. As the water evaporates, it leaves the mineral salts behind. After, of course, thousands of years, the intensity has multiplied.

Many archaeologists believe that originally the sea did not extend as far south as it does. We can see here a tongue of land that juts out into the sea. We know that the lower southern tip of the sea is very shallow. Many biblical archaeologists believe the ancient cities of Sodom and Gomorrah were located under this southern tip, and originally it was a very fertile plain, but a catastrophe caused the water to break through the land barrier and to flood south. There are signs of great earthquakes and other natural phenomena in the southern part of the Dead Sea. Today the Jews have tried to bring life back to the shores of the Dead Sea. They are taking the salt out of the land. Today, you can see a few tomato farms around the shores of the Dead Sea.

Make your dramatic monologues live with a good sense of biblical geography. Have your biblical character relate to his or her own surroundings. Above all, do not make mistakes in geography. Often a good role play will be spoiled by having the character in the wrong place—the Sea of Galilee in Judea! Know something about the distances between places. How far was it from Jerusalem to Jericho? What was the terrain like along the road. Congregations can tell when you have done your geographical homework.

## Conclusion

We have seen that the person who does dramatic monologues should know what the Bible has to say about the character in question. As you now begin to formulate a biblical character, go to a good Bible dictionary such as the *Interpreter's Dictionary of the Bible* and look up your Bible character. For example, look up the name of Paul, a well-known New Testament figure. The dictionary article will allow you to get an overall feel for Paul's exciting life. You should especially notice major events in Paul's life—events that you should underline in your presentation. Next go to a good concordance and find a list of all the passages in the Scriptures where the character's name appears. It is very embarrassing to role play a character and leave out an essential Scripture passage. Tentatively, make an outline of the character's life. Break the outline down into the major periods of the person's life. For example, you might use the following outline for the life of Paul:

A. Early life in Tarsus,
B. Paul as a young man,
C. Paul in Jerusalem,
D. Paul's conversion,
E. Paul in Antioch,
F. Paul's missionary journeys, and
G. Paul's arrest and imprisonment.

Doing biblical research will not only assure accuracy but also will allow you to get to know the biblical character. You must get into the character's "skin," so to speak. Find four modern translations, as mentioned above, and read aloud several passages of Scripture representing major events in Paul's life. Take the story of Paul's conversion in Acts 9:1-9. Try to imagine how you would have felt in similar circumstances. You had tried with all your might to fulfill the Jewish law. Now, suddenly, your whole life has turned around, and you are a Christian. What would have been your thoughts?

Once you know the biblical material, begin to feel the world in which the character lived. Read about the cities that Paul visited. What were they like? What kind of work did people do? How did Paul travel? What was travel in the first-century Roman world like? Once you have this secure foundation, you can "flesh out" the character and add color to the presentation. For example, Paul will become real because you have taken the time to examine all the avenues open before you.

You would want to explore Paul's message, also. How did that message relate to the total biblical message. What role did Paul play in the hourglass figure discussed above? How can you, the interpreter, interact with Paul in a faith response. Read the role play on Paul in this book. Now you are ready to put on your costume and portray Paul to your congregation. Good luck on your pilgrimage!

## Notes

1. For a helpful discussion of this point see Donald Miller, "How to Study the Bible," *Introduction to the Bible* (Richmond: John Knox Press), 144-151.

2. This model was used by William E. Hull in a faculty address at Southern Seminary in 1965.

3. Vincent Taylor, *The Gospel According to Mark* (London: MacMillan, 1953).

4. George Caird, *The Revelation of St. John the Divine* (New York: Harper and Row, 1966).

5. Gerhard Kittel, *Theological Dictionary of the New Testament* (Grand Rapids: Eerdmans, 1964).

6. I am indebted for the hourglass figure to Arnold Rhodes, "The Message of the Bible," *Introduction to the Bible* (Richmond: John Knox Press), 73.

# 3

# Moses: The Call from Contentment to Conflict

One of your modern writers has said that Israel was born through Moses. If it were so, it was an unwanted pregnancy. It was never my desire to be a leader of the people. It was never my desire to be a prophet of God. All I wanted was to find peace, have my family, and be a good shepherd. I expected to live out my days in the desert. My childhood was a period of confusion with the Hebrews telling me I was a Hebrew and the Egyptians telling me that I was an Egyptian. I lived on edge, always tense until my anger exploded. In a fit of anger I killed, and I became a fugitive.

It was the best thing that ever happened to me. For there in the desert I found a family with Jethro, Zipporah, and soon my own children. My flocks and family gave me the first contentment of my life. Life was good. I was really enjoying life. Then God got into the act.

At a time when a man ought to be finding some peace in life, eighty years of age, God interrupted my peace. It was an ordinary day. At least, it began as an ordinary day. I arose as I had a thousand mornings just like that one. The night chill was just giving way to the warmth of the morning sun. The buzzing of insects mingled with the bleating of sheep and other familiar sights, sounds, and smells. It started like a thousand other days, but this ordinary day would become an extraordinary one. I was leading the sheep to pasture when I passed that mountain. How many times had I passed by that mountain? But it was different that day. A bright light on the mountain caught my eye. First, I thought it was only the reflection of the sun.

Then it looked like a bush aflame. The dry desert bushes sometimes burst into flame, but this one was different. It did not flame up and disappear. My curiosity got the best of me, so I turned aside and climbed up a little way until I came close to the bush that was burning but not consumed. Those desert bushes should go up instantaneously, but this one kept burning. I climbed higher. Soon I could feel the heat of the flame.

Suddenly, there was the sound of the wind. At least I thought it was the wind. Was I losing my mind? The wind seemed to whisper my name. "Moses, Moses!" I looked about to see who called my name. No one was there. It was out of the fire that the voice came. "Moses, take off your shoes; you are standing on holy ground." I was not a religious man, but this was enough to make a believer of the most skeptical of men. I wondered who this strange, mysterious desert god was. Was it a god of this mountain angered by my intrusion. Falling on my face on the rocks and sand, I lay trembling, filled with fear and wonder. I dared not look to see who it was that spoke. "Here I am," I stuttered. "Do not come any closer," the voice echoed against the sky, "and take your shoes off because this is holy ground. I am the God of your father, the God of Abraham, the God of Isaac, and the God of Jacob." I thought, *What in the world are You doing here in the land of the Midianites?* This was the beginning of my firsthand knowledge of the one, true Almighty God.

I had heard stories about Abraham, Isaac, and Jacob. I had heard stories about God calling them, telling them that they would be a special people, but I certainly had never felt like a special person myself or a part of any special race. How could any Hebrew have felt special living in slavery? The voice grew in intensity until it thundered. "I have seen the affliction of My people and have heard their sorrowful cries." "*My* people" echoed in my brain. "I am come down to deliver them out of the hand of the Egyptians, and to bring them into a good land flowing with milk and honey." The words overwhelmed me like a storm, but then I heard words that struck like lightening: "I will send you to Pharaoh in order that you may bring

My people out of Egypt."

I cared nothing for Israel now. I had tried to help the Hebrews when the Egyptian master had slain one. My thanks was being reported to the Egyptians and made a fugitive. Now, God was telling me to abandon my comfortable life and go back to Egypt. Running away crossed my mind. *A bush! You've looked into a fire. You've sat by a campfire at night and looked into the flame. You've looked at a candle and been captured by the hypnotic light.* I was afraid to run. I hoped I was dreaming, but the rocks pressing against my body and the heat of the flame convinced me it was all really happening.

Maybe I could talk myself out of the assignment. "Why me?" I asked. "What special abilities do I have?" In those days, I was not much given to speech. I spoke only when it was absolutely necessary. When a man lives in the desert with sheep, he doesn't do a lot of talking. "You, Moses! You are the one who must go speak for Me." I am not a good talker, Lord. Zipporah laughed at me when I got excited and stuttered. He had an answer: "Your brother back in Egypt, Aaron is a smooth speaker, he will talk for you," He said.

Well, who are You? The question was a silly one. "I am who I am." Now what did that mean? After all these years I am still not sure. He has proven to be whatever He wants to be. To me He was Friend, Father, General, whatever was needed to get the job done. No name can capture His essence.

The flame continued to burn until it seared my very soul; my mind was grasped, and I could not turn loose. I could not back away or leave that experience. It was an experience that changed my life. I didn't want to go. I couldn't go. But He said I had to go. I learned early in my experience with the Lord that He has a way of destroying excuses. Never once did one work for me.

Then there were the signs. A stick became a serpent, and I was supposed to pick it up by its tail. No man who ever worked in the desert and has been around serpents is going to pick up a snake by its tail. But I feared that voice—the mountain, the powerful One—more than I feared that serpent. When He said, "Pick it up by its tail," I picked it up by its tail. (This can be pantomimed effectively with humor but portray genuine awe; likewise, the leprosy episode.) That wasn't enough. "Take your hand and put it inside your coat." I put it inside my coat. "Take it out." I took it out. There it was, that horrible dread disease: my hand was covered with leprosy. My heart jumped, and my whole body trembled. I had seen what it could do to people. "Put it back inside." Nothing He said made much sense. I was afraid to do that. Anywhere I touched those white sores to my body, they would take hold. My entire body would be contaminated. I didn't want to do it. But again, I didn't know what He would do if I didn't. I, I put it back and slowly, fearfully drew it out, and (pause) my hand was whole again! This was no ordinary burning bush.

I tried to quarrel with Him. I said, I can't go; I said, I won't go. And He said, "You will go." I went. I took courage from the fact that One who could change my hand, covering it with leprosy, and in a moment clean the leprosy—One who could take a rod and turn it into a serpent, One who could work these miracles: the burning bush and speaking to me out of fire—would be a good One to have on my side. I gathered my family, loaded our possessions, and back into Egypt we went. We met Aaron as He had said we would. Aaron quickly agreed to be the spokesman.

Next stop, the house of Pharaoh. I felt wise and powerful . . . until I saw the mighty Pharaoh and his court. He had the power of life and death. The burning bush was not there. The voice was not there. It was just me and Aaron and a hall full of Egyptians. There were armed soldiers everywhere. Mean-looking old men mumbled among themselves. Pharaoh was there. There was no place to run. I'd come too far for that. So I said, Pharaoh, God says to let His people go. Pharaoh laughed. His laughter sent chills down my spine. Everyone laughed but me and Aaron. Please, Pharaoh, let God's people go, just for a little while into the desert to worship. Pharaoh said no. Pharaoh set out to show the world who was in charge. He poured it on the Hebrew people. He laid greater burdens upon them and demanded more and more from them. Guess who they blamed? God had sent me to be their leader. God had sent me to lead them to freedom, but they weren't mad at God. It was: "Moses did this to us." That was the beginning of a terrible lesson for me. Time and time again I learned that these friends whom God had given to me would cause me more problems than my enemies. The Israelite people, throughout my life, were a much greater burden to me than the Egyptians. Time and time again, I had to contend with rebellion, harping, and lack of faith on the part of the people whom God had sent me to save. It's no fun to be the leader of a group of people who don't want a leader. It's no fun to be symbol of faith to people who have no faith. I tell you what I wanted to do. I wanted to go back into the desert and take care of my sheep. He wouldn't let me do that.

Next came the plagues. Pharaoh was a worthy adversary for any man. He refused to bow to the will of God. Pharaoh's heart was hard. The water turned to blood, the flies came, the frogs came, the locusts came, and the darkness came; still Pharaoh resisted. But he was no match for God. The Lord brought him to his knees with the most horrible of all plagues: the death of the Egyptian firstborn.

We were set free to go out into the wilderness. As we left there and traveled into the desert, I had the same kind of feeling that I experienced when I first came before Pharaoh: a sense of confidence, a sense of power, and a sense that the mission was well on its way. My confidence soon faded. The sound of thunder in a cloudless sky soon made us aware of the chariots of Pharaoh bearing down upon us. Before us was the Red Sea; behind us were the forces of Pharaoh. We were trapped between the power of Pharaoh's army and the Red Sea with no place to go. I thought then as a great saint has said, and I have thought many times after that: *"God, it is no wonder You have so few friends when You treat them like this." What have You gotten me into now? Pharaoh's chariots are bearing down, the sea is before us, and there is no place to hide.* Then that voice came again, "Moses, this is all for My glory, that Pharaoh and the whole world may know that there is none like Me in all the earth. Raise up your rod." I raised up that rod. Before my eyes the sea parted. It was as if there were walls on both sides as we marched through the sea itself. We were barely on the edge of the tide when we could hear the thunder of the horses, the rolling of the chariots behind us, and into the same pathway came Pharaoh's men. As our people reached the higher ground, I lifted my rod over the sea at God's command, and the waters rushed in. Pharaoh's army was consumed. God delivered us, and it was to happen time and time again. Bitter water, and God said throw wood in: the water became sweet. The Amalekites came—much more powerful forces, trained forces, an army which we were not—but as I stood up on the mountaintop, arms raised in prayer (How many times was I to do that?), God gave His people victory. Oh, there were failures. But every one of those failures was a failure of heart and courage, a failure of will on the part of God's people, not on the part of God. God delivers His people.

Then came Sinai. God must have loved mountains. We spent a lot of time together on mountaintops. On the top of the mountain, God talked with me. Each time He talked with me, my life was changed. No person can talk with God, person to person, heart to heart, and not be changed by the conversation. On Sinai, God gave me laws by which we might live. I've never been more angry than when I came down from that mountain and heard those terrible sounds—sounds of idolatry. The people whom God had delivered were worshiping before a golden calf. I believe if God had not been so angry, I would have prayed that He destroy them. He was already threatening to do that, so I pleaded for forgiveness. I interceded with God and pleaded with God that He would forgive those sinners. Those who repented were shown mercy.

Each time, each struggle, each failure, and each disobedient act took a little more out of us; it took a little more out of me. It was not to be my joy to walk in the Promised Land. But I came to realize that when I—and when Israel—did what God told us to do, we overcame. God is always offering vistas to those who have a faith to follow. There is freedom and a promised land for those who trust God. It was not Moses, but God. You can be a Moses. Listen to hear if God is calling you by name. "Moses, Moses!" That's the way He called me.

Perhaps He's calling you right now to a special task, to new faithful-ness, or to new courage. Will you listen now for the voice of God? It is natural to be afraid, but if you will give God a chance, He will over-come your fears. Listen! Is it your name the wind of God whispers?

# 4
# Hosea: Love that Costs

Oh, God, could it be her? No, it's not possible, not after all these years, but, those eyes, how terrible she looks. That woman has been ravished by the world. She's nothing but skin and bones; oh, the lines in her face! That woman must be much older—much older than Gomer. It couldn't be her. And yet, something in her eyes, shame perhaps, cries out to me.

Could that girl I married so long ago, that sweet, innocent girl, the girl with the dancing eyes and the long hair, could it possibly be her? Could a woman do anything to herself—let others do things to her—that would leave her in that kind of condition? Oh, God, it is her, isn't it? It's the girl that I married. It's the girl who betrayed me and left me. She has been ravaged by her foolish choices.

What should I feel? I should hate her. I should hate her for what she did to me. I should hate her for what she did to the children. I should despise her; I should laugh at her now and be glad to see her in the shape she's in. Shouldn't I feel good about the fact that she has come to this end, a wretched slave, mocked, and the object of lewd remarks? No one wants her now.

God, she did it to herself, I didn't do it to her, You didn't do it to her. She chose that way. Lord, how should I feel? What should I do? Why don't I feel happy about her suffering? Why can't I rejoice that I have been avenged? It hurts so much! When I took her to be my bride, I was the happiest man in the world. She was the prettiest woman in the whole village; yes, she was a flirt, but her flirtation was cute in those days. There was an innocence about it that made it appear less than evil. I thought that we would have a wonderful life together, that our love was strong enough to keep us both happy. It lasted . . . oh, it lasted for just a few days. She didn't want to be married to a preacher. She didn't like all the talk about God, she said, and justice and righteousness were boring subjects. She didn't want a husband who went around declaring the failures of others. She didn't want a husband who was the spokesman of God to call back her friends from their wicked and sinful ways. She didn't want to be the preacher's wife. She wanted a man who would be the life of the party—not a party pooper. At least, she wanted me to enjoy her being the life of the party.

She complained early of boredom. But I thought, *She'll get over it. Somehow she will come to love God as I love Him,* but she didn't. I often went away to preach and came home to hear her complain bitterly about the trips and my being gone. When our son was born, I thought this would be the answer. Who could help but love that beautiful child? Even though it wasn't the best possible world for him to be born into, I thought he could make a difference, at least for me and Gomer. I believed that we could provide for him a safe and happy home in which to grow. I should have known. I should have known how it would turn out when I returned and found her in a drunken stupor, the baby crying, and herself unkempt. From that time until the last time I saw her, it seemed that she was always drunk. How could one woman consume so much wine? No matter what I did to try to keep her away from it, someone always provided it. She found it somewhere. Then, a second child, a beautiful daughter, was born—but not mine. Another son, but he, too, was not my child. God, I tried to be patient, I tried to be loving, I tried to encourage her. I forgave her! She laughed in my face. She didn't want forgiveness from me or from You. She didn't think she needed any forgiveness.

It grew worse. I had to stop traveling and stay home with the children because I would come home and find them alone and unattended. When I came home one night and found her with another man, in our bed, with our children nearby I couldn't stand it. I begged her: you must stop this way of living, you cannot go on this way, you're destroying the children! You're destroying yourself. You're destroying me. STOP IT! For God's sake! STOP IT! She laughed hysterically. "All right," she said, "I'll stop it. I can't stand it here anymore. I can't stand you! I can't stand your preaching. I can't stand these snotty-nosed children. I can't stand this stinking place. I'm leaving." Where will you go? I asked. "There are lots of places for me to go," she said. "There are men who appreciate a woman like me. There are men who would rather dance and sing than preach. There are men who will buy me nice things. I deserve silver and gold." She said, "I want rubies. I want to go every night to a feast. I want to dance under the moon. I want to drink wine. I want to eat raisin cakes. I want to enjoy life. There are many men in the world who will buy me fine garments and give me all that I want to satisfy the desires of my heart."

Then she left. She was right. There were men willing to pay dearly for her favors. The next time I saw her she was dressed in a fine garment; she had a necklace and beads around her neck, all different colors. Silver bracelets hung on her wrist. Gold earrings adorned her beautiful little ears. She had cut her hair, her beautiful long hair that I had so loved. Many would have thought her beautiful, but I preferred the simple beauty of her youth. I didn't see her again for a long time, but there was always someone to tell me about her. Gossips throughout the land seemed to revel in tormenting me with their reports of her wildness. She had many lovers, it seems. She moved from town to town until finally I heard of her no more.

The children and I struggled along to make it the best that we could. But, God, You know how every night I lifted her up in prayer. Lord God, I prayed that You would watch over her and protect her. Apparently, You didn't choose to protect her from herself. And behold, what has she come to now? I've seen other women on the auction block but never one that looked so terrible or touched me so deeply. The lewd remarks of the men who stand around laughing, jeering. They don't want her. She isn't attractive to them anymore. There are no beads, no earrings, no necklaces, and no bracelets, not now. Her clothes are tattered, her hair is long again and matted. The auctioneer just pinched her arms and spoke of her ability to serve a man, to sweep his floors and clean his house. He actually patted her on a place where no man should touch a woman in public and spoke of some joy yet to be had. He's jerking her mouth open and showing her teeth like he would if he were showing a beast of burden. How horrible! Her appearance is more obscene than anything the men in the crowd could say or do. All she will bring is the minimum price of a slave.

God! What shall I do? Shall I stand at the edge of the crowd and tell her that she has gotten what she deserves? Shall I declare that what she's experiencing is Your punishment, Lord? Shall I join the mob in mocking her as a harlot? Shall I try to use her as an example to others and tell them this is what happens when people don't obey God, when they violate His covenant? Shall I use her as an example of what sin does to a person? Shall I proclaim that this is the way the wicked world uses people up and throws them away? She really isn't worth anything to anyone now. No beauty is left to attract the lewd men. I wonder how much she laughs now? There isn't even a twinkle in her eyes. Oh, God, what has she done to herself?

Lord, You know it will take every coin we have in this house to buy her. Even that small price will tax my meager resources. It will be this month's grocery money. Is it the best thing? Lord, I can't help it, it's the only thing I can do. Lord, You know that I love her. And that even now I want her back. Lord, help me, help me to restore her. Help me to use my love to make her again the person that she could have been. I will go, and I will pay the price. I will bring her home, not to be a slave in my house, but I will bring her home to be a wife to me and a mother to my children. I will say to her, "Woman, no longer will you play the whore. You must now be a wife, you must accept my love, and you must act as one who is loved." Lord, I will say to her, "Gomer, you will come home with me. You will dwell in our home for as long as you live, but you will not ever play the harlot again. Nor shall you have any man but me. And so, I will also be to you. Gomer, I covenant anew with you even as I did when we were first wed. You be faithful to me, and I will be faithful to you. And I will share the goodness of God's love with you."

*(Turns to leave, stops, turns back, and looks up.)*

What, Lord? Yes, Lord. I see it now. The experience that I have had with Gomer is like Your experience with Israel. What You have called me to say to Israel, Lord, is what I will say to Gomer. The devastation of Gomer is just like the devastation of Israel. As she has destroyed herself, and her beauty has been replaced by ugliness, so has Israel's. There is swearing, lying, stealing, murder, and adultery in this land. Violence is everywhere. The land itself mourns. The beasts of the field, and the birds of the air, the fish of the sea languish and disappear. It isn't Your fault, God; it is their fault. They have rejected the Law. They have rejected Your way. They have broken the covenant with You even as Gomer broke covenant with me. They, too, Lord, have gone after their lovers. They, too, Lord have been seduced by the promises of pretty things that don't last. Israel has adorned herself with the gifts of her vulgar suitors, and Israel has played the harlot even as Gomer did.

And yet, Lord, as I cannot give up Gomer because of my love for her, You will not give up Israel because of Your love for us. You would not destroy us but heal us. You are willing to receive unfaithful Israel back, even as I am willing to receive unfaithful Gomer back. As I shall seek to heal her and bind up her wounds, You will heal Israel and bind up our wounds. You, too, Lord, would require of us the faithfulness that You promised to us. As I loved Gomer in my youth, You loved Israel in our youth. You called us into being. You taught us how to walk. You held us in Your arms. You protected us with bonds of love, and we ran away. God, we do not deserve Your mercy, but we praise Your love. God, I will tell Israel of Your love. I will tell Israel how You're willing to buy her back from the slave block. I will shout to all that You will love us freely and heal our apostasy. I will tell Israel that we can dwell in Your house again, Lord. Your love is overwhelming. Now, forgive me, Lord, but I must hurry. I must hurry to deliver Gomer. And then I must hurry to tell Israel that You will deliver us. Where is that grocery money?

# 5
# Reflections of a New Mother

It has all happened so fast.
Can it really be nine months since my world
was turned upside down?
Less than a year ago my head
was filled with the normal thoughts
of a girl my age betrothed to
a fine man like Joseph.
I wondered if I could be a good wife.
Would he be pleased with my cooking,
with my care of his home?
What would it be like to leave
parents and family?
What would it be like to lie
with a man?
These thoughts were enough to
make me tremble.
Now here I am a mother, and still I
don't know what it is like
to lie with a man.
But I do know that Joseph is
a wonderful man—a kind and
attentive husband. He is a

man of faith and will be a
wonderful father for our Jesus.
Not in my wildest dreams could I have
imagined the strange events
of the last year.
I was alone in a garden praying
when it began.
Suddenly there was a man—at least he
looked like a man—who said he
was the angel Gabriel.
His words sang like the sounds of
the birds in a spring wind.
Was I dreaming?

"Hail, O favored one,
The Lord is with you!"

My heard pounded. I was sure I was
dreaming. I could feel my cheeks
turn red, and tears rose in my
eyes. It was no dream.

"Do not be afraid, Mary," he said, "for
you have found favor with God.
And behold, you will conceive in
your womb and bear a son,
and you shall call his
name Jesus.
He will be great, and will be called
the son of the Most High;
and the Lord God will give to him
the throne of his father David,
and he will reign over the house of
Jacob for ever;
and of his kingdom there will be

no end."

His words made no sense. In my confusion
I blurted out my doubt:
"How shall this be, since I
have no husband?"

He spoke of a strange marvel which I
cannot explain but which
has come to pass.

"The Holy Spirit will come upon you,
and the power of the Most High will
overshadow you;
therefore the child to be born will
be called holy,
the Son of God."

His words left me trembling but I found
myself accepting his strange prophecy.
"Behold," I said, "I am the handmaid
of the Lord; let it be to me
according to your word."

Holy, the Son of God? Could it be?

The thoughts were too great for me. I was
anxious about what Joseph and my
parents would think. When I told
Joseph, I could see the doubt and
frustration in his face. Who could
believe such a tale? My heart nearly
broke when he spoke of a
quiet divorce. My bed was flooded
with tears as I prayed and cried
all through the night.

It was like new life when Joseph

arrived the next morning to
say that an angel had appeared
to him in a dream. He did not
understand, but he believed.
Sweet Joseph begged my forgiveness,
but our first real embrace made words
unnecessary.

Real joy burst forth in me only when
I made the visit the angel had
instructed me to make to Cousin
Elizabeth. Her exuberant words
set my soul aflight, and praise
leaped from my lips:

"My soul magnifies the Lord,
and my spirit rejoices in God my Savior,
for he has regarded the low estate
of his handmaiden.
For behold, henceforth all generations
will call me blessed;
for he who is mighty has done great
things for me,
and holy is his name.
And his mercy is on those who fear him
from generation to generation.
He has shown strength with his arm,
he has scattered the proud in the
imagination of their hearts,
he has put down the mighty from their thrones,
and exalted those of low degree;
he has filled the hungry with good things,
and the rich he has sent empty away."

When Joseph and I set out

for Bethlehem to be
enrolled for Caesar's tax
census, I had no idea
my time was so near.

A long day on the back of a
donkey filled my body with
aches and my heart with
fear.

"No Room!" The innkeeper's words
brought tears to my eyes
and sobs to my lips. Joseph's
pleading got us a place in
the stable. There in the warmth
of the air among the animals
was Jesus born.

The poor animals were undoubtedly
filled with terror by my screams
and heavy breathing as my
body painfully sent forth the
One of whom the angel
spoke.

He looked so ordinary!
Joseph and I laughed at
His red bottom, long funny
fingers and toes, and His
wrinkled face like a
dried fig. But He is
beautiful. The struggle
of birth is now gone from His
precious face, and it radiates
the innocence of new life.

Can it really be? Will He save His

people? Can One so tender and
helpless reign from the throne of David?

Joseph says the words of the prophet
were about our—GOD'S—child:

"For to us a child is born,
to us a son is given;
and the government will be upon his
shoulder,
and his name will be called
Wonderful Counselor, Mighty God,
Everlasting Father, Prince of Peace."

For now, it is for me only sweet
little Jesus boy, but, Lord,
let it be to me and to Him
according to Your word.

# 6
# The Good Samaritan
# Luke 10:25-37

I was on my annual trip to Jerusalem and Jericho to sell my pottery wares. I always dreaded these visits for such a spirit of hatred existed between Samaritans and Jews. Yet it was very necessary for my business for me to make the trip every year to Judea. The Jewish businessmen did like Samaritan pottery—if not the Samaritans. Let me explain this age-old hatred between my people and the Jews.

Back in the year 722 B.C. on your calendar, the Assyrians had conquered the old northern Jewish state of Israel, whose capitol was Samaria. The Assyrians transported the ten northern tribes into captivity in other lands and resettled Israel with foreigners. My ancestors were in these foreigners. They eventually adopted the Jewish religion, but they were never accepted by the Jews in Judea. Following the fall of Jerusalem in 587 B.C. to the Babylonians, many Jews spent a long period of captivity in Babylon. When they returned years later, these Jews were led in rebuilding the Jewish temple by Ezra and Nehemiah. The Samaritans went down to aid in the rebuilding project, but all our help was rejected. In fact, the Jewish leaders asked all men with Samaritan wives to divorce them and send them home.

We Samaritans proceeded to build our own temple on Mount Gerizim. We accepted the five books of Moses as our basic law and observed the Jewish festivals and traditions. The Jews felt that we had stolen their religion and hated and despised us all. We, of course, developed the same hatred for them. In the Jewish law, it even says that a Jew could not take food or water from an unclean Samaritan. Of course, a Jew should never marry a Samaritan. During the reign of Coponius (A.D. 6-9), some Samaritans went down to the temple in Jerusalem, slipped in, and threw human bones all over it. The temple was unclean for days, and no Jew could enter it. They have never forgiven us for that trick.

Well, now you can understand why I always dreaded my annual trip to Jerusalem and Jericho. Jerusalem was not so bad. The worst part of the trip was the eighteen-mile journey from Jerusalem to Jericho. The Jews called this road "the valley of the shadow of death,"— for obvious reasons. The Jericho road transversed some of the most hostile land in Judea. You start out in Jerusalem at 2,500 feet above sea level, and eighteen miles later you arrive at the lowest point on the face of the earth: Jericho, 1,250 feet below sea level, near the Dead Sea. In just eighteen miles, the road drops off over 3,000 feet. The road winds its way through the Judean wilderness among the rising sand dunes. Hidden caves are situated along the way. Many persons in trouble with the Roman officials find this an area in which to hide. Thieves and robber bands also lurk in the hills.

The Jews travel in caravans and large groups. Even then, they never leave Jerusalem or Jericho after noon for fear of being caught on this dangerous road after dark. Well, let me tell you what happened to me one day on that road. I had tarried too long in Jerusalem with my business. It was well past noon when I left the city traveling eastward to Jericho. I knew it would be dark before I reached my destination. Being a Samaritan, I knew I could not join a Jewish caravan for protection. I hoped that perhaps I would catch up with one and stay a few yards behind it for safety.

I hurried as fast as I could. Every shadow scared the wits out of me. Suddenly, I couldn't believe my eyes—somebody was lying in the path ahead of me. Perhaps the person was dead—the victim of one of the nearby robber bands. The thought ran through my mind that I should hurry past the person and not get involved. He was probably dead anyway. As I drew nearer, I saw the man was bleeding, most of his clothes had been taken, and he had been severely beaten. I just couldn't pass him by! I ran over and turned him over. He spoke a few words to me—then I knew he was a Jew! I ran back to where I had left my donkey to fetch some oil and wine. I ran back to the man to pour this on his severe cuts and wounds. I bound up his wounds and placed him on my donkey and took him to a nearby inn.

The next day, I took out two denarii, about two days' wages for me, and gave them to the innkeeper. I asked him to take care of the wounded man until I returned in a few days on my way back to Samaria. I told him to provide whatever the wounded man needed and put it on my account.

Later in the week, I returned to the inn and found the wounded man doing much better. He introduced himself to me as Simon, a Jew from Jerusalem. Simon told me that he, too, had set out from Jerusalem past noon. He also could not find a caravan to join. He must have left about forty-five minutes ahead of me. Simon said that he was nervous and frightened as he rushed down the road. Suddenly, a group of men jumped him from behind a large rock beside the road. They beat Simon severely, ripping off his clothes and taking his money as well as his donkey laden with farm produce to be sold in Jericho. They left him in the road to die.

Simon said that when he regained consciousness, the robbers had gone. He heard the hoofbeats of a donkey coming down the path from Jerusalem. Surely, someone would stop and render aid. He saw, out of the corner of his eye, a man dressed in priestly white. Simon thought perhaps a leader of Judaism would stop and help him. But, no, the priest passed hurriedly by on the other side. Simon said that he tried to call out to him but couldn't.

Simon and I agreed that the priest did not stop because he had just been to Jerusalem to serve his two weeks in service to God in the temple. Over 10,000 men served as priests in Judaism. Thus, they were divided into courses that served only two weeks out of the year. Over 60 percent of the people in Jerusalem made their livelihood in connection with the temple. This priest had been on the mountaintop with God in Jerusalem. Now he was on his way back to his home in Jericho; all his friends and neighbors would stand in awe of him and wait upon his many stories concerning his stay in the temple.

If the priest had touched a dead person, he would have been unclean for days and would have found no welcome in his home village. He would have been the victim of shame rather than a man of honor. The Jews believed as did the Samaritans that a man should have nothing to do with the dead—even to walk by a cemetery. They claimed that women brought death into the world, so the women are responsible for preparing the dead for burial. Village women would be called in to wash the body and sprinkle perfumes upon it. The Jews do not believe in embalming. Widowed women are hired to mourn during the time of grief. The louder they cry, the more money they get paid. You can hear a Jewish funeral from a mile away. "You see," Simon said, "why the priest could not stop."

"I was so terribly disappointed," Simon exclaimed. "I thought that I would probably die there in the middle of the Jericho road." "Then," he said, "I heard the sound of more hoofbeats coming down the road. This time I saw a Levite from the corner of my eye. Yet, he too passed quickly on the other side of the road." Over 10,000 Levites serve in the Jerusalem temple. They provide the music and open and close the gates. This Levite had just finished his service in the temple and could not risk touching a dead man alongside the road. The Levite, too, would have been unwelcome in his home village.

"Then," Simon related, "a few minutes later I heard more hoofbeats coming down the road. Out of the corner of my eye, I saw you on the donkey. I knew you were a Samaritan by the way you were dressed. I knew for sure I was a 'goner'—you would be the last person to stop to help a dying Jew." But I did—I said quickly—you were my neighbor.

I later told my experiences to Jesus when He was preaching in my country of Samaria. Most Jews in traveling between Judea and Galilee would cross the Jordan River and travel up the eastern bank to avoid going through Samaria. Jesus went through Samaria. On one occasion He met a Samaritan woman at the well of Sychar. She came back to our village and told us of this Jesus. We were astonished that Jesus had spoken to a woman—a Samaritan woman at that—one who had five husbands. We all went to the well to hear Him preach.

Jesus often used my story to illustrate the cost of being His follower—we must have a broader definition of the word *neighbor.* A neighbor is not just a person who looks like us, dresses like us, or lives like us. Our neighbor is anyone we meet who is in need. Being a neighbor often involves a risk. The thieves on the Jericho road could have still been lurking in the nearby caves. I was very vulnerable in stopping to render aid. In your world, many of you use the excuse that it is too dangerous to stop and render aid anymore. People can even be murdered on the streets in front of your homes without anyone going to their help.

Since I have been in your country, I have noticed the thousands of street people. They go unnoticed by countless rich Americans as they rush to work. Your land abounds with many riches; there is no excuse for poverty and the homeless. Some of the harshest words I ever heard Jesus utter were directed against the rich. For a rich man to enter the Kingdom, it will be like a camel going through the eye of the needle. The poor people of the world are also our neighbors.

I was considered an outcast—I was a Samaritan. Any Jews hearing Jesus tell my story would have expected a Jewish layman to have been the third person or the hero of the story. How surprised they were when a Samaritan like myself became the hero of the story. It was like a black man being praised in a white Southern town or a Mexican being lauded in a Texas border town. Your neighbor doesn't even have to be the same color as you or of the same race. Such a broad definition of the word *neighbor* is costly. However, the kingdom of God demands such a price. The next time you ponder the word *neighbor,* remember what happened to me on the road to Jericho.

# 7

# Judas: The Plan that Failed

*(This entire piece is played with great emotion, at times bordering on hysteria. The speaker must sustain the tension while maintaining control. A solo rendition of "Judas," words and music by Billie Hanks, Jr., [Hope Publishing Company], will help to set the mood.)*

It wasn't supposed to end this way. I never meant for it to end this way. If only He had listened to me. If only He had taken my advice. Poor, sweet Jesus; poor, naive Jesus who would not listen; poor, foolish Jesus—now, He hangs from that ugly Roman cross. Do you think that I, I of all the persons in the world, would want to see any Jew hang from a Roman cross? Least of all Jesus? He just didn't understand the world. He didn't know how you change the world. If only He had listened to me, Jesus could be sitting on a throne now instead of hanging from a cross—if only He had listened to me.

I don't understand. Do you know what it's like? To be a slave in your own country? Do you know what it's like to have the boot of an oppressor on your throat? Do you know what it is to have your own priests and leaders betray you? I'm tired, so very tired. If I could rest, could think—too late for that now. If only He had listened to me.

In the beginning it seemed so right. I believed He represented what I had wanted for all my life. He was the *One,* the One who would set Israel free. He was the One who would return to us our dignity. He was the One who would lead us to drive the Roman oppressors from our soil. When first I heard Him, in Nazareth at the synagogue, He spoke the words of the prophet: " 'The Spirit of the Lord is upon me,/ because he has anointed me to preach good news to the poor./ He has sent me,' " Jesus said, " 'to proclaim release to the captives/ and recovering of sight to the blind,/ to set at liberty those who are oppressed.' " That is all I wanted: to set free the downtrodden, to release the captives, and to bring good news to Israel. I wanted people to see, to see the possibility of freedom, and to see our bondage. Jesus said then that He would fulfill that Scripture. It seemed possible. If only He had been able to see the world as it is.

I was certain He was the One for whom we'd waited; I was sure that He was the One around whom the people would gather. Everyone liked Him, in the little villages and everywhere we went; even the Samaritans and the foreigners would have been willing to help us. We could have thrown the Romans out. Each evening I would whisper in His ear: "When? Jesus? When? Jesus?" And He would smile and say, "The kingdom of God is here." Yet everywhere we went, there were still Romans—Roman soldiers, Roman rule, Roman this, and Roman that. It was grotesque to imagine the kingdom of God and Roman rule existing together. Jesus didn't understand!

Oh, we had always had preachers in Israel. There had never been a time in my life when one couldn't find a preacher on every corner of Jerusalem and every step of the Temple. There was always someone interpreting the Law. Throughout the countryside, there was always someone who was calling himself Messiah, someone declaring that he was going to set the people free. But Jesus, Jesus was different. He did things no other man has ever done. I confess, I don't know how He did it. There was a time when I thought that the hand of God was upon Him because the miracles He performed were not possible for an ordinary man. He produced the signs of Messiah. But if that had been true—if He had been the Messiah—He wouldn't hang now from the cross, would He? God would not have let that happen.

Oh, Jesus, why didn't You listen to me? I saw Him . . . I saw Him give sight to the blind, hearing to the deaf, speech to the silent. I saw

Jesus touch lepers and make them whole again, give strength to use-less legs and arms. I saw Him do things that no man had ever done. I don't know how He did it, but I saw Him raise the dead. If only He had listened to me.

You understand what it takes to change the world. It takes power, arms, troops, and force, but Jesus didn't understand that. When I tried to tell Him, He wouldn't listen. Jesus, Jesus, Jesus! If only You had listened to *me*. The words that had thrilled me were followed soon by words that frightened me. It shook me to the very center of my being. He said words strange to the lips of any man in Israel but particularly to One who would be Messiah. He told the crowds that it used to be said, " 'An eye for an eye and a tooth for a tooth.' But I say to you, Do not resist one who is evil." And when someone slaps "you on the right check, turn to him the" left also. Who does that? Who in his right mind would not resist evil? What man would allow someone to strike him on one check and turn the other? As if that wasn't enough, Jesus said, "Love your enemies and pray for those who per-secute you." Who among you does that? Who among you prays for their enemies? Who among you loves their enemies? Who among you returns good for evil? Poor, blind Jesus. If only He had tried my way.

I never could quite understand some of the things He did: too much time wasted on children; too much time fooling around with broken bodies and broken minds when the whole nation was broken. It was much more important to be about repairing and healing the nations than fooling with individuals. But I never could get Jesus to see that. He always had time for others. Once when the children wanted to come to Him, and we tried to protect Him—He never rested long or cared for Himself enough, so we were sending the kids away—He rebuked us. " Let the children come to me," He said. It was always "Let them come." Let everyone come!

When He was not wasting time with children, it was women. A man like that should never speak to a woman in public, let alone in-vite them to sit with men and be taught the things of God. He even allowed the women to follow us. He not only spoke to them; He actually touched them.

Jesus was so simple, so naive. He just didn't understand. There were so many missed opportunities. On one occasion He had been teaching all day, and there had been some healings. The day was growing late. The children were bawling, and parents were beginning to fight among themselves. The crowd was restless. We said to Him, "They are tired, they are hungry, and we are tired and hungry. Send them home." And Jesus said to us, "Feed them." "Feed them?" I was the keeper of the purse; I knew that we hardly had coins enough to feed ourselves, let alone that crowd. Later, some said that there were as many as 5,000 men there plus all the women and children. The whole hillside was covered. Andrew brought to Him a little boy with a few loaves and fishes. Jesus blessed those loves and fishes, and we fed every person there until their bellies were full. *Now,* I thought, *people would follow someone who can feed them; now is the time, if only You would speak the word. This multitude, these men, would follow You to Jerusalem. We could drive the Romans out.* "Jesus," I said, "speak the word, and they would become an army." He looked at me, shook His head, and whispered, "Judas, you don't understand." It was *He* who didn't understand! He just couldn't face reality. If only He had listened to me.

Why wouldn't He listen to me? I was the smartest one of the bunch. I was the shrewdest one, I was the most aggressive one, of all the twelve, and yet Jesus was always rebuking me. I loved Him, in my own way. I didn't always do stupid things like Peter; I wasn't always bickering like Andrew and John, always groveling like some. And Levi, ha! A tax collector! Betrayer! Jesus took him into the group and treated him just like all the rest. Opportune moment after opportune moment passed without action. Jesus sounded more like a religious fanatic every day. He had to be reminded that our faith was one of national pride and power. David's throne must be reestablished. Then the world would know Israel's God. Something had to be done. In some way, I had to get His attention. In some way, I had to bring it all to a head, I had to make something happen. I had to bring the will of God down. Surely Jesus just didn't understand the situation. I would force Him to see and act.

There were so many missed opportunities. There was one at Bethany when we were on our journey to Jerusalem—where I hoped He would throw out the Romans. He sent us to get a donkey. We brought back this small animal. He climbed upon its back. How silly He looked; His feet nearly touched the ground. If I had known why He wanted the beast, if only He had told us what He wanted, I would have gone into Jerusalem and stolen for Him a fine Roman horse with a great chariot, and He could have ridden into Jerusalem like an emperor, like a king, and like a Messiah should. But not Jesus. Jesus chose a donkey, the beast of burden. Nonetheless, it was amazing what happened. As the animal began to move toward Jerusalem, the multitudes began to cry out, "Hosanna! Hosanna! Hosanna to the Son of David! Blessed is he who comes in the name of the Lord! Blessed is the kingdom of our father David that is coming! Hosanna in the highest!" (John 12:13; Matt. 21:9; and Mark 11:9-10). "The kingdom of our father David"—they knew, they understood. He was the only One there who didn't act like He knew the Messiah's role. They would have followed Him. Once again He let the moment pass. I knew then I had to help Him: I had to make Him do what He would not do, I had to force Him to see what He would not see. I would make Him a Messiah!

I would make Him a Messiah like David. I could force Him to do what He should do. I began to plot. The next day we were still in Bethany and went to the home of Simon. There, a woman burst into the room. Women again! He often wasted time with women. Once He had sat down with a Samaritan woman and drunk from her jar. It's bad enough to converse with the Samaritans but a Samaritan *woman*! He had spoken to her in public. There were always women hanging around, following Him. It's not that I object to women in their place, you understand. But on this occasion, there was a woman of the streets—a woman that no man should have spoken to in public, least of all a teacher of Israel. She had with her an alabaster vase full of costly perfume. She broke the vase and poured it over Him. She is wasting that, I cried out. Don't You know, Jesus, that this perfume could be sold, and with the money we could feed the poor? Jesus did not rebuke her. He rebuked me! He said, "Let her alone, she has done a good deed." Again I realized that He would never do the appropriate thing. He wouldn't be the leader that He should be. I determined at that moment that I must carry through with my plot. I would make Him see.

I went to the chief priests in order to betray Him. I felt dirty, I hated to be in the presence of those traitors to Israel, those people who collaborated with the Romans. But, you see, I had to do it! I had to do it. I agreed to betray Jesus. Yes, Yes, they gave me money, but it wasn't the money. I didn't do it for the money; I took the money back and flung it in their faces. I had to make it appear that I really wanted to help them and betray Him.

That night we gathered in an upper room. It was a strange evening. We had been together so often, but on this particular evening there was a shadow over us all. Hardly anyone spoke above a whisper. After a few minutes, Jesus arose and took a basin of water and began to wash our feet. He acted like a common servant. Who would follow a man who treated women as well as men and washed the feet of His followers? Who would follow a man that chose to ride into the Holy City of David on the back of a donkey? You understand, His way wouldn't work! You must resist evil with force. Then He spoke of betrayal. I thought, *He knows! Someone has told Him. Perhaps one of the priests,* but each of the others cried out, "Surely it is not I, Lord." He looked into my eyes and pierced my soul: "Go," He said, "What you are going to do, do quickly."

I knew where He would be. So I went and told the high priest where Jesus could be found. I didn't want to go with the soldiers to arrest Him, but they insisted. It was part of the deal, they said. I had to point Him out. I had told them earlier that it would be the one that I would kiss. As we approached the garden, I could see Peter, James, and John. They were doing what they did best: sleeping. They jumped to their feet, and foolish Peter drew his sword and cut off the ear of one of the guards. But Jesus, as I might have expected, rebuked Peter and healed His enemy. Who heals His enemy? They came to arrest Him, and He did not resist, but He even healed one wounded in taking Him. I approached Jesus. My hands trembled. Once again, His eyes looked into my soul. How hard it was for me, but I had to do it. I had to do it! (Pause, speaking softly and slowly.) I betrayed a friend with a kiss. And as my lips touched His cheek, I could taste the salt of His tears and perspiration. I could feel His soul trembling. I didn't want to do it. I had to do it.

You understand. Don't blame me unless you would have done it differently. I ask you, where were the others during this trial? Where were the others when they dragged Him through the streets, humiliated Him, whipped Him, and scorned Him? Where were the others when they nailed Him to a cross between two thieves? Where were those to whom He had given sight, those to whom He had given hearing, those whom He had made whole? Where were the parents and friends of those whom He had healed and of the ones He had raised from the dead? Where were the thousands He had fed that day? Where were they when the Romans nailed Him to a cross? Where were you? Where were *you* when they nailed Him to that cross? Would you have cried out, would you have defended Him? You see I thought that everyone would rally around Him. I thought in that moment of physical danger He would forget all of His words of peace and call forth His friends to fight. But not Jesus. Poor, dumb Jesus—if only He had listened to me—It was His own fault.

Don't judge me! Don't you judge me unless you would follow a leader like Jesus. I ask you (dripping sarcasm): Do you love your enemies? Do you pray for those who abuse you? Do you bless those who curse you? I ask you: Do you turn the other cheek? Don't judge me unless you can live by His words and live like He lived.

Oh, God, I betrayed a friend with a kiss. God, what have I done? Oh, God, let me die, let me die! (Runs down the center aisle of the church and out into the night.)

# 8
# Peter: A Slow Learner

The sea is soothing. Here in this quiet place, one can remember, can dream, and dream again the dream once dreamed, the dream I lost and found again. The dream has become a vision that is the force of my life, a dream not yet fulfilled, but a dream that I know will be fulfilled.

It all happened so quickly, so long ago. At first it was like a pleasant dream from which one awakes too soon. Then there was the terrible experience of the nightmare that suddenly became reality. I wanted to awake and find that it was all the creation of the mind. But it was real and true. I am running ahead of myself. It is hard for me to do that when I look back: excited by the past, thrilled by the future, the promise of the Lord who is ever with me.

My life was empty, meaningless. It was as if I lived on a wheel that turned in the same circle every day. I lived—existed I should say—a life of endless repetition, arising each morning to go down to the boat to fish, to bring in the haul, and to come home again. I was not a religious man; indeed, there was nothing which gave my life any meaning. Oh, I was a Jew by birth and practice. Holy Scripture had been taught to me as a boy, and, occasionally, I attended synagogue. Sometimes I even attended high feast days in Jerusalem. But it was not personal. It was a part of my national heritage. The important part of my life was only what I could do with my hands: only the fish and the selling of the fish. The day-in-and-day-out routine was all I had until that day.

Andrew persuaded me to come in early one afternoon to go and hear a strange new preacher, a weird character who preached in the wilderness. He was called John the Baptizer. This John was really stirring things up. I went, not out of any desire for spiritual teaching or healing. I went for the show. John stood on the seashore roaring like a lion. He spoke of judgment on the sins of the people and called for repentance. Suddenly, in the middle of his address John stopped. His eyes fixed on a man moving through the crowd. All eyes followed the gaze of John to look on this strange man.

I did not know who He was then. I did not know His name, where He came from, or anything about Him. As He approached, the roaring voice of John become a soft whisper like the wind. "Behold," he said, "the Lamb of God, who takes away the sin of the world!" It was, of course, Jesus, unknown to me then. Jesus approached and asked John to baptize Him. John refused. How strange! John had been pleading with people to come and be baptized; now one came, and John refused to baptize Him. Jesus insisted. John took Him down into the water and baptized Him. As His head emerged from the water like a child being born from a watery womb, a strange silence fell on the crowd, and suddenly a voice spoke from heaven, "This is My beloved Son, with whom I am well pleased."

We quietly went home. Andrew and I talked little about what we had seen or what had happened that day. That night I had trouble going to sleep, and when I finally drifted off to sleep, I was haunted by that scene—by the words which I had heard.

The next morning I awoke earlier than usual, had my breakfast, and went down to the boat. Andrew was already there. We looked at one another, but we did not talk. And just as we had begun to prepare for the day's fishing, Jesus appeared alongside the boat. He looked at us and said, "Come, follow Me, and I will make you fishers of men." I can't explain to you even now why I felt compelled to follow Jesus. Maybe I thought there could be some purpose in my life, something more than fish and nets, buying and selling. I followed Jesus.

Those early days were thrilling. Jesus healed the sick; He gave sight to the blind; He gave hearing to the deaf; He touched twisted limbs and straightened them. He spoke words of comfort, words of love, and words of assurance. He spoke not of condemnation, not of judgment, and not of repentance as John had spoken. Jesus spoke of the love and the mercy of God. Jesus reached out to people to whom no one had ever reached out before. Women followed Him, outcasts followed Him, sinners followed Him, lepers followed Him, and, yes, the curious followed Him as well. I saw all kinds of strange occurrences, but there was one day when an extraordinary thing happened. A crowd had gathered at our home. They had brought many people for healing. Jesus was teaching when, suddenly, there was a noise on the roof; rubble began to fall on our heads. My first thought was: *people will be hurt, and I'll be blamed.* I thought the house was falling. I looked up to discover a hole in the roof. Someone was being lowered into the room. The sun was bright through the hole, and I could only make out what looked like a sack of grain being dropped on us. When the pallet touched the ground, I saw a terrible sight. It was a man's body horribly misshapened. I thought even Jesus couldn't help this one. There was no way that those rotten limbs could ever be made whole again. Jesus spoke first of the forgiveness of that poor creature's sin. That brought a murmur from the crowd. Which would be easiest, to forgive the man's sin or heal him? Jesus looked at him, prayed for him, reached out, and touched him. It was as if new life flowed through his veins like some miraculous liquid, and each particle flew through the man's body; the limbs were straightened until he was made whole! Jesus said to him, "Rise, take up your pallet and go home." And that man picked up his pallet and walked out of there whole!

I could tell you of other such occurrences. There was the time by the seashore. We had been there all day, and the people were tired—we were tired. We came to Jesus and said, Jesus, the people are becoming restless, they are hungry. Let us send them home so that they may eat. Jesus looked at us and said, "Feed them." Feed them? How could we feed them? We had not enough bread for ourselves let alone for this multitude of people. He turned to us and asked, "Is there no food at all?" Andrew spoke up, "There is a lad here who has five barley loaves and two fish." Jesus said to bring the lad to Him with his bread and fish. The boy willingly handed over his food. Jesus prayed, blessed the bread and the fish. "Distribute the food," He said. We did! We fed five thousand that day ! There was food for everyone, and when we had finished and collected what was left, enough was there to last our band and the little boy's folks for many days. Miracles! Miracles! This One could make broken bodies whole, misshapen limbs straight; this One gave sight to the blind and fed the hungry.

No other man like this had ever lived before on the face of the earth. He was different. There was talk by some that He was the Messiah, but I knew that could not be true. After all, the Messiah was to be like David. The Messiah was to come as a mighty warrior—a soldier. The Messiah was to come in power and majesty and might. Jesus fulfilled none of these things. Oh, I wondered and thought about it, and then there was that day at Caesarea Philippi. As we sat around the fire, Jesus asked the group, "Who do the people say that I am?" And one said, "John the Baptist; but others say, Elijah; and others, that one of the old prophets has risen." "But who do you say that I am?" Without thought, the words leaped from within my being as if someone else had taken control, and I did not really hear what I said until the words flew from my lips. You are the Messiah, the anointed one of God. Jesus looked at me and said, "Blessed are you, Simon Bar-Jona! For flesh and blood has not revealed this to you, but my Father who is in heaven." How proud I felt. He said that He would no longer call me Simon. From that day forward I was to be "Rock." My spirit soared.

I was soon humbled. Jesus began to speak of going to Jerusalem to die. No, Master, you will not die. No, Master, it will not be so! "Get behind me, Satan!" He said softly. I did not know—did not understand, couldn't grasp—what that meant. How could I know? From that day, we moved toward Jerusalem. The days grew increasingly difficult. Everywhere we went, Jesus was challenged by other rabbis. It was obvious that the scribes were trying to trap Him. In each crowd there was some hostile, critical voice. There was more quarreling within our group. Jesus seemed to grow increasingly somber.

I thought when we arrived at Bethany that a visit with Lazarus, Martha, and Mary would lift His spirits. What happened was totally unexpected. He sent us to obtain a donkey. We followed His instructions and brought the beast back. He mounted it and began to ride toward Jerusalem. The streets filled with people, and they began to shout acclamations. "Hosanna to the Son of David! Blessed is he who comes in the name of the Lord!" How they shouted for Him. They put down limbs from nearby trees before the animal that carried Him. Some took off their cloaks and laid them down before the animal. It was a magnificent, glorious moment. It was a royal parade worthy of the Messiah. That evening we were exhausted. We went to a special place and had a very special meal.

We gathered around the table. Jesus spoke of death again and of betrayal. He said that one of us, one of the twelve, would betray Him. *No,* I thought, *that is impossible.* Each in turn cried out, "Is it I, Lord?" "Is it I?" "Is it I?" Judas rose and went into the night, hardly noticed. It was only later that we realized why he left. Jesus, I said, you can count on me! You can count on the Rock. I will never betray you. I will never deny you; you can count on me, Jesus! His words chilled me. "Before the cock crows, you will deny Me three times. " A chill gripped me; I shuddered in disbelief. *He is wrong this time,* I thought.

He asked me, James, and John to go with Him to the garden of Gethsemane to pray. It had been a full day. Our bodies were worn out. We were to remain at the gate while He went in to pray. One after the other, we fell asleep. The stern voice of Jesus awakened us. "Could you not watch" and wait a little while? Lord, the spirit is willing but the flesh is weak. "Watch," He said, "and pray." We did not know what we were waiting for, we did not know what we were watching for. Never had He been so angry and agitated. He went into the garden. A second time He awoke us from our slumber. The third time He did not have to awaken us because the noise of the crowd aroused us, and we found ourselves surrounded by the priest's guards led by Judas. Judas rushed up to the Master and kissed Him. The soldiers moved to arrest the Master. I drew my sword and tried to defend Him. I sliced off the ear of one of the priest's soldiers. Jesus rebuked me. He touched the ear and healed the man. He healed one who had come to lead Him to His death. It made no sense to me. They took Jesus away, and we fled for fear that they would take us, too.

I was frightened. I didn't understand what was happening. I followed the soldiers and Jesus at a safe distance to the courtyard of the High Priest. I wanted to know what they were going to do with Jesus. I wanted to hear what we were supposed to do. But I tell you I was scared. I thought they would take all of us, throw us in prison, maybe kill all of us. One of the girls who was serving came through the courtyard. She looked directly at me. "You are one of His followers," she shouted. Don't be silly, woman, I am no follower of His, I said. Trembling, I moved over from the edge of the courtyard to the fire. I extended my hands to warm them at the fire. The serving girl came to the fire, looked at me and said, This man is one of them, he is one of the followers of Jesus." One of the men spoke up and said, "You are a Galilean." I cursed. I cursed and fled from that place. In the distance the sound of the cock announced the dawn. The crowing of the cock announced not only the dawning of the morning but the betrayal and denial of Jesus. You know those horrible events that followed: Jesus ridiculed and humiliated, Jesus nailed to a cross. Jesus suffering inside and out. Jesus' hands pierced. Jesus' side pierced. You know all that story, that horrible, horrible story! And there was nothing I could do!

We gathered again after it was over—after the crucifixion. After they had taken Him down, and He had been carried to the tomb of Joseph of Arimathea, we gathered to try to pull ourselves together and see what we could do. What was there left to do? On the morning of the third day the women went to the tomb. After only a short period of time they returned. "Jesus," they said, "is not in the tomb. Jesus," they said, "has risen. He is alive." We could not believe it. John and I looked at one another and ran. John outran me to the tomb. It was empty! The tomb was empty! My mind began to spin. Was it really possible? Could He be alive? Soon, others told of seeing Him. I heard and saw no one. I despaired. He would never trust me again. My betrayal had earned rejection. I decided to return home, to the sea. We went fishing. We caught nothing: we fished all night and caught nothing. In the morning, there was a strange shadowy figure on the seashore. He called out to us. We should have known then for the voice said, "Boys." Who could call men like us "boys"? "Boys," the voice said, "cast the net on the right side of the boat." I cast the net on the right side, and it was soon so filled with fish that we could hardly pull in the net. I knew that voice. I knew that figure. Then John said, "It is the Lord!" I jumped over the side and swam to the shore as rapidly as I could. I discovered when I arrived at the shore that He already had fish cooking and bread prepared. Soon the others joined us. We did what I'd thought we would never do again—we shared a meal together. When the meal was finished, Jesus lay back, looked at me, and said to me, "Simon, son of John, do you love Me?" How could He ask such a question? "Yes, Lord; You know that I love You," I said. "Feed My sheep," He said. And a second time, this time His voice pierced my heart. "Simon, son of John, do you love Me?" The blood rushed to my face. I could not believe He would ask that of me again. "Yes, Lord; You know that I love You." He said to me, "Feed My sheep." A third time, His voice a sharp sword touching the center of my being. He asked, "Do you love Me?" The tears flowed freely down my flushed cheeks. My stomach felt as if I would explode. How it grieved me that a third time He questioned my love. My response this time came thoughtfully, painfully, slowly from the depth of one who wanted to be the Rock. Yes, "Lord, You know everything; You know that I love You." "Feed My sheep."

It was years before I came to realize all that this meant. Now I can tell you, my dear brothers and sisters in Christ, that my joy is fulfilled in Christ Jesus, my Lord, only when I feed His sheep. We love Him by feeding His sheep. The sheep are all those for whom He died. Some are in the fold, some wandering outside. We love Him by loving them. We serve Him by serving them. The question comes loudly to His church: "Do you love Me?" "Feed My sheep."

# 9
# Encounter with Caiaphas

I am Caiaphas, high priest of the Jews. I hold the most important role in Israel. I served as High Priest from A.D. 18 to A.D. 36 as you reckon time. Thus, you will probably remember me best as the one who ruled over the Sanhedrin during the trial of Jesus. It was a great day in my life to be appointed high priest by the Roman procurator: Valerius Gratus. To be high priest, one must please the Romans.

The role of high priest is both a political and religious office. The office involves ruling over the Jewish supreme court composed of seventy-one Pharisees, Sadducees, and other priests. This court resolves political as well as religious cases. When the Romans took control of Judea, they also began to influence the Sanhedrin. They eventually took the vestments which I wore yearly into the holy of holies and locked them up. If I did not perform my political duties as the Romans demanded, I did not receive these vestments. The Sadducees especially try to play political games with the Romans. Of course, I know very well which authorities I should try to please.

My most important function is to administer the worship activities of the Jewish temple in Jerusalem. Over 20,000 priests and Levites serve in the temple. There are so many that each person serves only two weeks out of the year. The priests and Levites are divided into twenty-four courses, each course serving one week, twice a year. The other weeks of the year, they work at various hand trades in their home villages. I, of course, remain in Jerusalem at all times to oversee the temple activity.

Let me tell you more about our temple. As you probably know, it was built by King Solomon in 950 B.C. Hundreds of years later, it was destroyed by the Babylonians in 586 B.C. The Jews were in captivity for many years in Babylon, and the temple lay in ruins. After the Jews returned from captivity, Ezra and Nehemiah led the efforts to rebuild the temple. Finally in 515 B.C., it was finished. However, all the Jews broke out in tears on the dedication day because it was not nearly as beautiful as Solomon's. The returning Jews just did not have the money to restore it to its former splendor. In 20 B.C., Herod the Great started an effort to remodel the temple. Many non-Jews call this the third temple, but we Jews would never give that kind of glory to Herod. We still speak of it as the second temple. This remodeling was finally finished after my rule in A.D. 66. A few years later the Romans would level our beloved temple to the ground in the Jewish uprising of A.D. 70. The temple would never stand again after that. In your day, if you should visit the temple area in Jerusalem, you will find the Arab temple there called the Dome of the Rock.

Thus I serve in the so-called second temple even as the remodeling work continues on. The temple complex is made up of a series of interlocking courtyards. My most important task is to wall off the precincts where God dwells so that no unclean person would draw near. The temple is located on an extended platform on top of Mount Moriah in Jerusalem. This area covers thirty-six acres. So you can see, the area is indeed a very large one.

Let me take you on a walk through the various courts of the temple. You enter the temple through many and various gates leading from the city of Jerusalem into the sacred courts. Let us enter through the Golden gate facing eastward toward the Mount of Olives. The first court we enter is called the court of the Gentiles. Any non-Jew can enter this part of the temple. We must be careful not to touch a Gentile, or we will have to go home and take a ritual bath. As you see, this court is surrounded on all sides by colonnaded porches. To the south, you see the beautiful two-storied porch called the royal porch. To the east, you can behold Solomon's porch. It is said that Solomon sat there and supervised the construction of the first temple. The porches are decorated with the Greek columns typical of Herod's time.

The very important temple activity takes place in the court of the Gentiles. All the money brought into the temple has to be exchanged into temple currency. We have tables set up throughout the court for this purpose. The money changers sometimes charge 10 percent interest for that service. These profits go directly into the temple treasury. We also have animal inspection tables set up in the Court of the Gentiles. All animals brought to the temple for the purposes of sacrificing must be inspected to assure that they are free from every spot and blemish. Any tainted animal is rejected, and the worshiper must buy one from the inspector. Sometimes the temple price will be double that of the market price.

Jewish worshipers must be particularly careful not to touch a Gentile as they proceed through the court of the Gentiles headed for the Jewish inner courts. If you touch a Gentile, you must return home and take a ritual bath. I know of one instance in our history where a high priest was spat upon by a Gentile, and he could not enter the holy of holies that year. You must remember, however, that we have been very generous to provide a special place for worship in our temple even for the unclean Gentiles. Overlooking this court on the northwest corner is the fortress of Antonia. Over 2,000 Roman soldiers are stationed there. The Romans can go up into its five-storied towers and observe what is going on in the whole temple complex. Every year at Passover, some political uprising will take place in the court of the Gentiles. The Roman guards will rush in through a secret passageway leading from the fortress into the court and put down any trouble.

The Jews pass on through the Gentile court and enter through the gate beautiful into the main Jewish part of the temple. Over this gate, you see a beautiful frieze of a grapevine representing the nation of

Israel. A wall with a warning sign tells the Gentiles not to proceed any farther into the temple on penalty of death. One must also climb several steps to go to this next level of the temple. Many beggars line up at the gate hoping to receive some alms from the pious Jewish worshipers. It is written in Jewish law that one must give to the poor.

The next court is reserved for the women. This court is also surrounded by columns, but it is much smaller than the Gentile court. In addition, four small rooms can be seen—one in each corner of the court. In the upper right-hand corner is a room reserved for the lepers. In our day and time, any skin rash is considered leprosy—even mildew on the wall. Inside this small room, there stands a pool for bathing after all signs of leprosy have departed. In the lower right-hand corner, one can see the room for buying wood for the sacrifices. In the upper left-hand corner is the room where oil is also sold for the services. In the lower left-hand corner stands the room reserved for the Nazarites, a group that has pledged not to cut their hair or drink strong drink for a special religious purpose. Around the walls of the courts are thirteen trumpet-shaped vessels for the depositing of the offerings. Thus the Jewish temple treasury is located in the court of the women. All women, girls, and boys under twelve must remain here with their mothers. Other unclean Jews, male and females can go no farther into the temple. This is true especially of someone with an issue of blood, a leper, or someone who has been mutilated in some way.

At the end of the women's court, one can see the fifteen steps leading up to the Nicanor gate. These steps are most important in Judaism. All unclean Jews must stand here to receive their cleansing. The lepers after they have washed in the pool will come here to receive their bill of cleansing to be taken home to their village rabbi. Mothers stand here after childbirth to offer up a sacrifice for their cleansing—after forty days for a male child, eighty days for a female child.

The men and boys over twelve leave the court of the women and proceed up the fifteen steps into the court of Israel. The Levites stand along the steps and play their trumpets. The gate to the court of Israel is then closed. This court is a very narrow one with only a wooden railing separating it from the court of the Priests. The men hand over their sacrificial animals to the priests. Laypersons are not allowed to proceed any farther than the wooden railing. The man of the household offers up the sacrifice for the whole family. Before marriage, women must adopt the religion of their fathers and after marriage the religion of their husbands. On special feast days the court of Israel is crowded with thousands of worshipers.

The court of the priests lies behind the wooden railing. Only those of priestly lineage can proceed beyond the railing. A large swimming pool structure dominates this court. This structure is called a laver and rests on twelve bronze oxen—three facing each direction of the compass. All animals to be sacrificed must be washed in this pool by the priests. Beyond the laver is the large altar of sacrifice, one of the most important structures in the temple. It stands some fourteen feet tall. The priest goes up a ramp to the top of the altar where he sacrifices and burns the animals. The blood of the animal is thrown against the foot of the altar. Sacrifices are offered here around the clock.

On the preparation day for Passover, 20,000 lambs are sacrificed on this altar in one day. A pipe runs from the foot of the altar down to the nearby Kidron brook. This allows the blood to run off from the altar. In the year before the fall of Jerusalem to the Romans in A.D. 70, Josephus reported that Jerusalem was surrounded by the Roman army—no one could go in or out. The people of the city were so hungry that some ate their own children. Yet the sacrifices continued daily at the altar of sacrifices.

Beyond the court of the priests looms the three-story main temple building. It is the only part of the temple with a roof over it. All the other courts are open air, for it very seldom rains in Jerusalem. The temple building is divided into two rooms. The first room is called the holy place. One must go up steps, across a porch, and then part a veil in order to enter this room. The room contains a seven-branched menorah, a table with twelve loaves of bread, and an altar of incense. It is quite an honor to be selected to serve in this court. When the priests arrive in Jerusalem for their two weeks of service, I always select the oldest of the priests to receive this honor. Younger priests might have to serve in the court of the women or the court of the lepers. The priest chosen would burn incense on the altar several times a day. This is where Zacharias heard the news that he would become a father even though he was advanced in age.

Beyond the court of the priests stands the holy of holies, the most sacred spot in Judaism. I, alone, as high priest of the Jews am allowed to part the veil and enter this chamber once a year. The holy of holies is cubical in shape and kept bare except for the ark of the covenant. It contains the Ten Commandments of Moses. On the Day of Atonement, usually in late September or early October, I part the veil and enter the holy of holies. For twenty-four hours before entering, I am locked up in an adjacent room so that I will not become unclean in any way. Before I enter the holy of holies, a chain is placed around my leg so that if I drop over dead, I might be pulled out without anyone else entering the chamber. On the day I enter the holy of holies, I take the blood of a goat and sprinkle this on the top of the ark of the covenant. This atones for all the sins of the Jews for that year. I also have special vestments which I wear into the holy of holies. Since the Romans conquered our land, they keep these robes locked up and do not give them to me unless the taxes have been paid for that year.

After staying in the holy of holies for about thirty minutes, I exit the sanctuary and take another goat called the scapegoat and place the remaining sins of Israel upon that animal. It is then taken into the desert and thrown over a cliff. It is a most exciting day as you can well imagine. I am the only one in Israel worthy to part the veil and enter the holy of holies. Of course, I keep all 613 laws of Israel perfectly!

The trouble with the new Christian religion is that they break down the walls of division and let classes of people mingle together. As high priest, I have sworn to keep the unclean away from God's sanctuary. Walls must be built to seal off the unclean people. We all know that God is a holy God, and only the holy can come into His presence. You Christians make so much of the veil of the temple being rent during the crucifixion of Jesus. Christians interpret that to mean that now all people can enter the holy of holies and that a priest is no longer necessary. It makes me cringe to think that any person, no matter what condition in life, might enter the holies of holies. If you Christians were to follow our system, you would keep the unbelievers in the outer courts; the women would be segregated in their courts along with other unclean people. The men should have their own place of worship where they can be apart from the women. Then you should have a place just reserved for the preachers apart from the laymen. Finally, only your greatest preacher should be allowed to enter into God's presence. He should wear a special suit and shoes reserved for that time.

I find that I have many areas of disagreement with Jesus and Paul—especially Paul's words in Galatians 3:28, "There is neither Jew nor Greek, there is neither slave nor free, there is neither male nor female; for you are all one in Christ Jesus." I would call upon you, as my parting words, to keep the walls erected and keep the holy of holies sacred.

# 10
# Pilate: Pragmatist

(*Speaking off stage*) No, tell them I will not see them. I am sick and tired of the whole affair. Oh, these Jews! Uncivilized barbarians! What a week they have given me. I am exhausted, physically and emotionally. How I hate these Jews and their coarse land. This weather's so hot. It is always hot here. How I long for the cooling breezes of the Mediterranean blowing across beautiful Rome. Will I ever have a decent post again? Will I ever be allowed to enjoy the beauty and pleasures of Rome? How could they send me to a place like this? It has always been terrible. Is it any wonder that this place is populated by barbarians and atheists? The gods certainly cannot be faulted for not wanting to live here. Who would want to worship a god who would be the lord of this kind of land? It is not so surprising that these Jews worship only one God, some strange God of the desert, and deny the civilized gods of Rome and Athens, gods who act like men and understand the pleasures of this world. How I hate the Jews and their religion.

From the first, they have given me problems. When I arrived with my guards carrying the image of Caesar on their banners and marched into their temple, what a fury they made. It was open rebellion. I thought I was going to have to slaughter the whole bunch. Indeed, that is what I should have done. But I feared the censure of Rome, so I yielded and withdrew the troops; no longer do they carry the image of Caesar on their banner. Always compromise is required when dealing with pagans. You would think that these Jews with their strange ways would get along among themselves. Only one God, but they can't agree about Him. There are so many different religious factions, and always some new ones developing. They have the Pharisees, the Sadducees, the Essenes, and the Zealots. Oh, the Zealots! They are people I understand, dangerous revolutionaries. I respect them because they are willing to fight for their land. When they brought this little man from Nazareth to me, I thought that He was a Zealot, but He wasn't. He lacked the courage and violence of the Zealots. But I am getting ahead of myself.

It all began when that old fox Caiaphas came calling at the praetorium. The audacity of those Jews! They would not enter the palace because, they said, it would make them ceremonially unclean for their great religious festival that was to occur in a few days. I accommodated them and came out on the porch to meet them. Who is this fellow, why have you brought Him to me? (*pause*) Oh, yes, I have heard tales of this preacher from the hills, this miracle worker. What does that have to do with me, or Rome? Why bring Him to me? It was the death penalty they wanted, and they could not condemn a man to death. But surely they did not want the death penalty for someone who simply disagreed with their religious beliefs? How ridiculous to quarrel over religion to the point of bloodshed! What is the charge against this man? I asked. He is an evil doer, they replied with great pomposity. Oh, take Him away and judge Him according to your own law. Then Caiaphas spoke, "We found this man perverting our nation, and forbidding us to give tribute to Caesar." "He is a traitor to Rome and to His own people." "He is a revolutionary who threatens to overthrow Rome." How could anyone imagine that this poor, pitiful man, so bedraggled looking, could be a revolutionary who would pose any threat to these men of power or to the city authorities? Who would believe that He could in any way be a threat for Rome? He claims to be king, they said. Oh, very well, bring Him before me. "Are you the King of the Jews?" Are you saying this on your own initiative, He asked, "or did others say it to you about Me?" Such insolence from a prisoner was astonishing. I'm not a Jew, Man! Your own people have delivered You to me. What have You done? "My kingship," He responded, "is not of this world." Well, if it is not of this world, we Romans aren't interested in it. This is the only world we know or care about. He remained silent. Look, Fellow, why don't You say what they want You to say, and they will let You go home. Why all this fuss?

I told the Jews quietly that I could see nothing wrong in this man. I couldn't understand why they insisted on blood. Again I asked Him, Are You a king? "You say" He said, "that I am a king. For this I was born, and for this I have come into the world, to bear witness to the truth. Every one who is of the truth hears My voice." What strange words coming from a Jew! It was the Greeks who were so concerned about truth, and we Romans have adopted their philosophy. I had never known a philosopher in Jerusalem. Oh, there had been some in Rome but not here. How strange to hear so common a voice speak of truth. Truth, truth is the concern of philosophers; truth is not the concern of politicians. "What is truth?" I asked. Again I told the Jews I could find no fault in Him. But they would not let go. They wouldn't let me go, they wouldn't let Him go. I was growing tired of the whole affair.

I took a recess to think about it. I removed myself to the sanctity and sanity of the palace. While I was in the palace, Procula, my dear wife, came to me and begged me to have nothing to do with this Jesus. She had had a dream. I, too, dream, I said, so what? I dream often. I dream of beauty, I dream of Rome, I dream of the pleasures of this world. I dream of being sent away from this godforsaken place. I could see she was serious. "I have been warned in a dream," she said. "Have nothing to do with that righteous man. He is an innocent and good man." I didn't listen to her. I couldn't listen to her. I thought the country was driving her crazy, and in these last few days she has been horribly depressed. I am worried about her, but perhaps if we can just get back to Rome, back home she will be alright. This barbaric place would drive any civilized person mad.

I returned to the Jews and their prisoner. I had conceived a plan to do the right thing and let all of us save face. You see, the custom was that I should release each year some prisoner to the people on the occasion of this special Jewish feast. What do they call it? Ah, the Passover, the Feast of the Passover. Yes, that's it. Each year at Passover I released a prisoner to them. I had a prisoner: a horrible man, a real revolutionary. This prisoner was a Zealot of the first order—a man with blood on his hands. He had killed not only Romans but Jews as well. He was the type of person that no one in their right minds would want set loose in their town. I ordered the guards to bring Barabbas to the porch. There on the one hand was this vile creature: this monster; on the other hand was this simple little man that they called Jesus, a man who from all appearances had done no wrong. I tried to avoid the priests. Speaking to the people I asked, Do you wish that I should release to you Jesus or Barabbas? Who will you have: Barabbas the robber, Barabbas the murderer, or the preacher from the hill country: Jesus. One voice cried out, "Barabbas, release to us Barabbas." Another voice, "Barabbas.", "Give us Barabbas." Soon the whole mob, as if a chorus, over and over again chanted, "Barabbas." I should have despaired by then, I should have had done with the whole thing. But I thought that perhaps I could satisfy them with something less than blood. I ordered that Jesus be taken by the praetorium soldiers to have their way with Him. These soldiers who hated this country and hated the people as much as I did were always anxious to have a Jew to beat up on. They took Jesus. They made for His head a crown of thorns, placed it on Him, and crushed it down until blood flowed down His face. They made sport of Him, hit Him, and spat upon Him; they scourged Him until He could hardly walk and returned Him to me.

How pitiful He looked now; He was so badly beaten you could hardly recognize His face. Surely that would be enough. Look, people, I said, I bring Him out to you that you may know that I find no guilt in Him. "Behold the man!" Surely you will set Him free. This time almost as if on cue, the chief priests and the officers cried out, "Crucify Him, crucify Him!" All the people joined in, "Crucify Him!" "Crucify Him!" I was tired of the whole thing. I would have nothing else to do with it. It wasn't my business, after all, it was their business. All I wanted to do was to maintain order. I didn't want to be involved to begin with. What did it have to do with me? It has always been my policy not to get involved, to avoid conflict whenever possible. It is the way of the wise politician. So I ordered that water be brought, I dipped my hands into the basin, and I rubbed them together *(pantomime the action)*. It was a symbol that I was washing my hands of the whole affair. I would sign the death order, but all of us would understand that His blood would be upon the Jews.

They took Him away. I had my own little joke though. I had a sign made, "The King of the Jews." Oh, that made the priests furious. Change it, they said, at least write upon it that "This man *said*, 'I am King of the Jews.' " I would have nothing else to do with it. I said, leave the sign alone. They dragged Him through the streets. I am glad I didn't have to watch it. I tried to keep cool, to be above it all. It really wasn't any of my business.

The mob joined with the soldiers to take Him to the place of execution, and there He died. His death was confirmed to me by my soldiers. They pierced His side, and water came out. There was no doubt that Jesus was dead. His death was probably accelerated by the beating and by all He had been through before they had ever brought Him to me. One of the citizens came to me, a man named Joseph, and asked if he and his friend Nicodemus could take the corpse and bury it. I gave my permission. Again, Caiaphas and his friends showed up at my door, vultures that they were. If they take His body and put it in a tomb, someone is liable to steal the body, they insisted. Steal the body, I screamed, why would anyone want to steal a body? They claimed some of His followers had taught that He said He would rise from the dead. Rise from the dead, I laughed, who would believe such nonsense? Another one of your silly superstitions that one would even think of the possibility of rising from the dead. If you want a guard, set your own guard.

That was four days ago, Now they have been back. They want to see me again. It seems the body has disappeared. They want me to order a search for those who stole the body of Jesus. I will have nothing else to do with it. I have washed my hands of the whole affair. Procula—I really believe she is suffering a mental breakdown—has told me that there are rumors in the city that this Jesus has risen from the dead. She says there are those who claim to have seen and talked with Him. What foolishness! You and I know that no one, not even a Caesar, can be dead and rise again. How I long for the sanity of civilization. If only I could wash my hands of the pettiness, the heat, the sand, and everything about this wretched place. No one will ever know about what happened here. I may someday tell my grandchildren about the poor carpenter King who had to die to satisfy His own bloodthirsty people. Well, I have the satisfaction that I did all that I could. No one can fault me for the handling of this case. I am free from all responsibility in this matter. *(Slowly rubs his hands together as if to remove difficult stain.)*

# 11
# Encounter with Paul

I, Paul, was born in the great city of Tarsus of Cilicia around 1 A.D. Tarsus was the fourth leading city of the Roman Empire with a population of many thousands. It had also a large Greek university in which Stoic philosophy was taught. Thus, I was born into no mean city! My parents had migrated to Asia Minor from the little village of Gischala in Galilee due to religious persecution. I have often thought that if they had not moved, I might have known Jesus as a boy. My father became very wealthy by making tents. He gave money to the Roman government for the beautification of Tarsus and was rewarded with Roman citizenship. Thus, I, Paul, was born a Roman citizen, a fact that would be very helpful to me in my later life.

My Jewish name was Saul. This would indicate to you that I was born also into a very pious Jewish family. I was named after the first king of the Jewish nation. I was also born into the tribe of Benjamin, one of the most outstanding of the Jewish tribes. It was required of every Jewish father that he teach his son the Law and also to work with his hands. Thus, I began to learn the 613 laws of Judaism as well as the skills of tent making. At eight years of age, my father sent me to the village rabbi to begin preparation for an exam which every Jewish boy had to pass at the age of twelve. Many Jewish boys learned to recite in Hebrew most of the Old Testament Scriptures.

The day I passed the exam was a very important one for me. Before, I had to sit with my mother in the balcony of the Tarsus synagogue. It was a big day in my life at the age of twelve when I walked with my father onto the main floor of the synagogue and became a "son of the covenant." I felt so good reading from the Torah before my elders. At the age of eighteen, my father sent me to Jerusalem to study with some of the leading rabbis of Judaism, such as Gamaliel. What a day in my life, when I arrived in Jerusalem and caught sight of the Jewish temple. Every male Jew dreamed of making this pilgrimage at some time in his life. Now, for several years, I would live in the major city of Judaism. I fell in love with the Law and wanted to pledge my life to protect and guard it. I wanted to become a rabbi myself. However, no one was allowed to teach until he reached the age of thirty, or old age. Hence, I journeyed back to work with my father in Tarsus until I should reach that age.

Looking back on it, I would have to say that those years in Jerusalem were very formative ones for me. I learned to appreciate God's divine law for the world. Finally, on my thirtieth birthday (around A.D. 30), I went back to Jerusalem to begin my career as a teacher. I arrived there just after the death of Jesus on the cross. I never had the opportunity to meet Him in the flesh. A group of His followers, called the people of "the Way," was causing some difficulty in Jerusalem. One of the leaders, a man called Stephen, had even taught that the Jerusalem temple was no longer necessary. I am ashamed to say that I participated in stoning Stephen to death. I stood nearby and held the cloaks of those who carried out the death sentence. I can still see Stephen's face in the back of my mind, even to this day. He cried out, "Lord, do not hold this sin against them." At the time, I could not understand how anyone could be so forgiving while he or she was being tormented.

When I was thirty-two, I got special permission to go to Damascus, Syria, to root out the Christians who had established themselves in the city. The journey on horseback took about two weeks. During that time, I had ample opportunity to reflect upon my years of persecuting believers in the Jerusalem area. Many times they would sing hymns as we were tormenting them. I think that deep down in my conscience I admired their courage and conviction. In my long years of study of the Jewish law, I had found no joy in my life. I knew that I was missing something in my relationship with God.

Just outside the city gates of Damascus, I suddenly saw a bright light, and I heard the voice of the Lord Jesus speaking with me, "Saul, Saul, why do you persecute Me?" I fell off my horse, and, suddenly, I lost my eyesight. The Lord asked me why I was persecuting Him. He then gave me the commission to go the Gentiles and share with them the good news. I was led blinded into the city of Damascus to the house of Judas on the street called Straight. After several days, the Lord sent Ananias to me to restore my eyesight. The Jews, however, were very jealous of me and plotted to take my life. During the night hours, the local disciples lowered me in a basket over the city wall, and I fled into Arabia for many years. There I worked through this new experience that had happened to me, and I also did some missionary work among the people who lived there.

After three years, I went up to visit with the Jerusalem church and to meet the apostles. These people felt that they were a little better than I, for I had not been one of the original twelve, and none of them had been a persecutor of the church. A young man by the name of Barnabas stepped up, introduced me to everyone, and became a lifelong friend. After talking with the Lord's brother, I was encouraged to leave Jerusalem, for I had too many enemies there. I decided to return home to Tarsus and work with my father once again. I was thirty-five when I left Jerusalem.

I labored with my father for nearly seven years. During this time I preached among my own people. Even as a Pharisee, I had been a zealous missionary. However, sadly I could never win over my own father and mother, and much pressure was placed upon me to take a wife. Among the Jews, a boy was expected to be married by sixteen and raise up many sons to honor God. Girls were usually married at thirteen, had nine or ten children, and were dead by twenty-five. Life was very tough in my time. The ancient world had no teenagers—one was either a child or an adult. Our world could not afford the luxury of those in-between years that you call adolescence.

I chose to devote myself to the Jewish law when I was sixteen years old. Thus, I was never married. In my time, a whole society of Jewish men called the Essenes lived by the Dead Sea and devoted themselves to the Jewish law. They were permitted to remain unmarried. Even after I became a Christian, I remained unmarried because I thought the Lord Jesus might return at any moment. I needed to devote all my time to preaching the gospel and reaching as many people as I could.

One morning I was working in my father's shop when I heard a knock at the door. I opened it and beheld the face of my old friend Barnabas from Jerusalem. He said, "Paul, a new church has come into being in Antioch of Syria. All the members are Gentiles, and they need someone with your background to lead them—someone who can get along with the Jews in Jerusalem but yet relate to them as Gentiles. They really need you! Will you go with me at once to Antioch?" I was forty-two years of age as I said good-bye to my mother and father and journeyed with Barnabas to Antioch. I would never be home again for any length of time.

We arrived in Antioch, one of the leading cities of the Roman Empire, with a large population. A small church had come into being with about forty members—mostly slaves and ex-slaves. We met in a cave on the edge of town. There was a back exit in case we had to make a hurried departure. We would often meet at sunrise on Sunday morning for our worship services so that the slaves could hasten home and cook breakfast for their masters. Sometimes we would meet late in the evening. This church had such a vision. The old mother church in Jerusalem had possessed the gospel for years but had not done a lot with it. They had kept it all bottled up in Judaism. This small group dared to dream that the whole Roman world should hear of Christ.

I remember one service very distinctly. We were all praying. The members began to file around us and place their hands on our heads, praying that God would send us out as missionaries to the whole Roman world. We took up the charge—Barnabas and I—and decided to leave in a few days for Barnabas' homeland of Cyprus. Barnabas wanted to take along his young relative: John Mark. A few days later, we made the journey down to Seleucia on the coast of Syria and caught a ship sailing for Cyprus.

It was so exciting as we sailed into the port of Salamis on the coast of Cyprus. I was forty-seven as we started this first missionary journey. We went into Salamis and began to preach in the main city square. I must say it took a lot of courage to stand up and start preaching about a God that the local Greeks and Romans had never heard of. Yet, we did it! Many people began to show some interest. Then, we decided to walk across the island to the capital of Paphos. We were eager to reach more and more people with the gospel.

In the capital city, the Lord really blessed us and gave us the opportunity to preach to the Roman governor of the island, one Sergius Paulus. He was very receptive to the gospel and believed. His court magician, Bar-Jesus by name, grew jealous and tried to interfere with our preaching. The Lord struck him blind! Within a few days, we decided to take a ship over to the mainland of Asia Minor and preach there. We landed in the port city of Perga. Ahead of us stretched a road that would lead 100 miles up through the mountains into the province of Galatia. It was a dangerous road filled with all kinds of hazards. I couldn't believe it, but John Mark came to me and said that he wanted to go back home. The road ahead was too filled with danger, and Mark was a bit homesick as well. I never could stand a quitter! He wouldn't listen to reason and sailed on back to Jerusalem where he was responsible for spreading the tale that we were converting Gentiles without forcing them to be circumcised. This would cause us a lot of trouble when we got back home.

Barnabas and I headed up the long road into Galatia, arriving in the important city of Antioch of Pisidia. We immediately went into the synagogue and started to preach the gospel to the Jews. We always tried to reach our own people first. The Jews grew jealous, so we had to leave Antioch and journey on down the valley to the cities of Iconium, Lystra, and Derbe. In Lystra we met some Jewish people by the name of Lois, Eunice, and Timothy. They were all converted to Christ. Finally, after nearly two-and-a-half years, Barnabas and I traveled back to Antioch of Syria to give our report. The journey had been full of dangers and threats, yet we also had made a great impact with the Christian gospel.

I wish you could have been there in the service as we gave our report to the church at Antioch. There was hardly a dry eye in the whole place. Everyone was amazed that there had been such receptivity to the gospel. Trouble, however, was brewing! The church at Jerusalem summoned us to come to visit with them and to prepare a defense of our gospel. Some in the mother church were distressed that we were converting Gentiles without asking them to undergo circumcision and to become a Jew first. I have always felt that John Mark must have spread that word around. Have you ever noticed that every time a great revival breaks out in the church, there is always trouble brewing somewhere?

Barnabas and I journeyed down to Jerusalem and over the next days gave a defense of our gospel. Even Peter, who at times was a bit "wishy-washy," stood up and spoke out on our behalf. Along with James, the Lord's brother, we finally worked out a compromise with the Judaizers in the church. I agreed that we would take up a collection for the poor in the Jerusalem church among the Gentile Christians. We would also teach them certain of the moral laws of Judaism. The Judaizers, in turn, agreed that we could bring the Gentiles into the church as they were with no obligation to follow the law of circumcision. Later some of these same Judaizers went back on their promises and gave me a lot of heartache. They would follow me around, enter a church after I left, and teach the new converts that circumcision was necessary. I later wrote the Galatian church a letter against these people.

We journeyed back to Antioch, and Barnabas suggested that we take another missionary journey since the first had been so successful. He also indicated that he wanted to give John Mark another chance. I said that I did not want to take along that quitter again. Barnabas got a bit angry and left for Cyprus with John Mark. I selected a new traveling companion, a fine fellow by the name of Silas. I suppose good came from our disagreement, for now the Lord had two missionary teams instead of one.

Silas and I traveled across the land route through the Cilician gates to revisit the churches that we had made in Galatia. We stopped in Lystra and visited Lois, Eunice, and Timothy. Young Timothy decided to go along with us on the journey. We certainly needed as much help as possible. The three of us continued the trip on to Troas, near ancient Troy on the coast of the Aegean Sea. The legendary beauty Helen once lived there, and that's where the story of the Trojan horse took place. I wanted very much to move up into northern Asia Minor, but during the night I received a vision of a man pleading for us to come over into Macedonia.

The next morning, we set sail for Macedonia and arrived shortly in the city of Neapolis, the port for Philippi. I was fifty years of age when I set forth on this trip into Europe. We would spend nearly three years on the road in Greece. We followed the famous Roman road, the Egnatian Way over the mountains to that famous Roman city of Philippi. Philippi had been settled by Roman army veterans and was the most Roman city in Greece. Latin was the dominant language in the city streets. I could not find a Jewish synagogue in the city, so on the sabbath I went to the banks of a river just outside the city gate. There I met some women worshiping Yahweh; they were so-called God-fearers: Gentiles who worshiped the Jewish God but had not fully converted to Judaism. One of them, a woman by the name of Lydia, invited us to her home and allowed us to make it our headquarters while we were there.

While in Philippi, we cast the evil spirits out of a little slave girl, and as a result we were arrested and placed in jail. During the night, there was a great earthquake, and the doors of the prison came open. However, none of the prisoners tried to escape. When the jailer discovered this, he was so overjoyed that he listened to us preach. He and his whole household were converted. The Roman officials were distraught to find the next day that I was a Roman citizen and had been placed in jail without a trial. They encouraged me to leave town.

We journeyed on down the Egnatian road to Thessalonica and Berea, preaching among the Jews and the Gentiles. At Berea, I left Silas and Timothy to continue to preach as I sailed on for Athens. I was impressed there by the beautiful but pagan temples and buildings. I even found an altar to the unknown god, just in case they had overlooked any. I went up on Mars Hill and took on the Greek philosophers at their place of debate. They thought I was preaching two gods: Jesus and Resurrection; they just laughed at me. I did not have much success there and decided to leave for Corinth where Timothy and Silas would catch up with me.

The city of Corinth was sort of a combination of your New York and New Orleans. Over 500,000 people lived there. Even the Romans "looked down their noses" at Corinth. For a few months, I supported myself by making tents. Then I met Priscilla and Aquila, and they helped me in the work. After some two years of fruitful labor, I decided to journey back by way of Ephesus to Antioch. I was fifty-three years of age when I got back home.

Silas and I took one final journey over to Ephesus. I was fifty-four as I set forth on the trip. Ephesus was one of the leading cities of the Roman world. I decided that on this journey I would spend my time in one city and do an in-depth type of missionary work. Finally, after some two years of activity, a riot took place in the city among the silversmiths who sold small statues of their local deity, Artemis, to tourists. They became upset with my preaching against idol worship. They felt a direct threat to their business. They could not find me, so they dragged some of my friends into the great theater, and a riot started. After the uproar had quieted down, Silas and I left and traveled through Greece to revisit the churches we had brought into being. We then left Greece and stopped briefly by Miletus to say goodbye to our Ephesian friends and traveled on to Caesarea in Israel.

At Caesarea I was warned by friends not to go up to Jerusalem, for the Jews had decided to kill me. I had taken up a collection, however, for the Jerusalem church, and I wanted to complete the project. When I got to Jerusalem, I visited with James, the brother of the Lord, and he warned me also not to go into the temple. I went ahead anyway, and the Jews started a rumor that I had brought a Gentile into the court of the Jews. A riot started, and the Roman guards had to rush in to save my life by arresting me. I spent several months in the fortress Antonia in Jerusalem. A young relative of mine warned me that the next time I was taken from prison, the Jews would kill me. I warned the Roman commander, and during the night I was transferred to the Roman jail in Caesarea. I was fifty-eight at the time.

I remained there for several years during the rule of Felix and Festus. No charges could be brought against me. Finally, when King Agrippa had come to visit with Festus, I made the appeal that every Roman citizen could make—to go to Rome and be heard by Caesar Nero himself. I disliked setting out in the winter months since the Mediterranean could be so stormy, but the Roman commander hugged the coastline to avoid going out to sea. We stopped on the Isle of Crete to take on supplies. I begged the commander to stay there in port for the rest of the winter. However, he would not listen and set sail for the western side of Crete. When we left the harbor, a strong northeastern storm hit us, and we were blown all over the sea for nearly two weeks. The whole time I kept telling the commander, I told you so.

Finally, after some days, we found ourselves breaking up off the coast of the Isle of Malta. The soldiers wanted to kill us all, but I was the commander's friend, and he talked his men out of that one. He allowed us to jump overboard and swim on pieces of the wreckage toward shore. The local natives had built fires for us to warm by. I went out to help gather wood, when a great big snake bit me on the arm. Everyone stood around waiting for me to swell up and die. I surprised all of them and did not. The next spring, they put us on another vessel headed for Rome. I was sixty years of age when I reached there.

I remained in Nero's prison for some five years waiting for my case to be heard. While waiting I wrote many of my letters: Philippians, Colossians, Ephesians, and Philemon. Finally, Nero burned down the city of Rome and blamed it on the Christians. In the ensuing persecution, I was sentenced to be beheaded at the age of sixty-five. Looking back over my life, I would say it was well worth it. I have left a lasting impression on the development of the Christian faith. My letters were the first books to be written in the New Testament. If all of my letters were removed, there would be a big gap in your Bible.

Several lessons can be learned from my life. I always stepped out in faith. When the Lord called, I responded. I might have given in to fear from all the threats that I received. The call to follow Christ makes a radical demand upon our lives. It is a call not to look back but to look forward. This call caused me to break with all the traditions of my past. Even the law lost its powerful grip over me. I even lost contact with my own family and friends. The call of Christ may call you to tread down new paths of service. It may involve a summons to risk and to dare and above all to be obedient.

New doors of challenge also brought me new and exciting developments in my life. I became God's channel of mercy to the Gentiles. I would have never found that blessing if I had not found the courage to answer the call of God. Your call does not have to come in the same way as mine—bathed in bright lights. It may come in a still, small voice calling you to follow where He is leading you. You may find in that call the fulfillment of your life.

I must also say that the call of Christ also brings with it hardship and pain. Many times I suffered beatings, imprisonment, and pain. Yet the Lord always provided me the endurance to deal with it all. I eventually paid the greatest price of all—my life. In our Greek language, the word *witness* is *martus* from which you get the word *martyr*. To witness really means to stake our lives on what we believe in. I never allowed threats of death to block my testimony. The call of Christ may mean the summons to die! May my own pilgrimage of faith serve as an example to you.

# 12
# Timothy: Journey to Ephesus
# Revelation 2:1-7

PASTOR: Let us journey back in time and visit the ancient city of Ephesus. We have arranged a time capsule for us all to board. All aboard! Ah, we have arrived in Ephesus. Jason, the first-century mayor of Ephesus, has consented to tell us of its history and give us a personal tour.

JASON: Welcome to Ephesus, the greatest seaport of Asia Minor. Let me begin with a bit of our history. Legend has it that a group of Greek colonists went to the Delphi oracle to seek her wisdom in the founding of a new city. She related her assurances to the colonists that a fish and a wild boar would be their signs as they sought to locate the new settlement. They set sail on the Aegean Sea, looking for a suitable location. One evening they anchored their ship off the coast of Asia Minor and went ashore to cook their supper on the beach. As they were cooking the fish over the fire, one of the fish jumped out of the pan and landed in a bush; this, in turn, scared a wild boar that was hiding there, and it ran away. The colonists remembered the words of the Delphi oracle. They proceeded to found the colony of Ephesus on that location.

Whether that story had any validity, we do not know. However, these first Greek colonists came to the area around the eleventh century B.C. They expelled the local inhabitants who had worshiped Cybele there for many centuries and built their city between the mountains of Koressos and Pion, some distance southeast of the Hellenic Ephesus. The Greek colonists over the next four centuries gradually changed from the worship of Athena to the veneration of Artemis, the goddess of the local Anatolian population. Their greatest accomplishment was the building of a huge temple to Artemis at the beginning of the sixth century B.C. It was built on marshy ground to avoid damage from earthquakes. Historians in your day count this pagan temple as one of the seven wonders of the ancient world.

In 560 B.C., Croesus, king of Lydia, conquered Ephesus and brought it under the control of Anatolian power. He added to the temple to Artemis by extending the sanctuary and introducing golden calves for its beautification. The population moved from the hillsides down to the temple area and constructed homes there. In 546 B.C., Ephesus came under control of Persia and was deemed a part of the satrapy of Ionia. During political upheaval and feuding in the area in 450 B.C., the temple of Artemis was badly damaged. About a hundred years later, in 356 B.C., it was burned to the ground by Herostratos, a man looking for some way to write his name in history. Legend says it was burned on the very night that Alexander the Great was born.

In 334 B.C., Alexander the Great conquered Persia at the Granicus River, and Ephesus came under Macedonia power. The temple of Artemis was rebuilt to become again a very imposing structure. Let us stop and visit this temple. It is 425 feet long and 225 feet wide. There are 127 columns, sixty feet high, each constructed on its own pedestal. As you can see, thirty-six of these columns contain elaborate reliefs. A horseshoe-shaped altar, trimmed with marble, occupies the center of the temple. Many consecrated women serve in this temple.

Upon the death of Alexander the Great, Lysimachus became the ruler of Asia Minor and city of Ephesus. He is often considered the founder of the modern city. A story is told that Lysimachus built a wall around the present city. During his rule it was necessary to relocate the city, so a third Ephesus was built. The area of the third city was constantly being inundated by the river, with the whole area

being swampy and disease ridden. After the new city was constructed, Lysimachus found that the people were reluctant to move into it,
so he stopped up the storm sewers, flooded the old city, and the inhabitants were forced to take up residence in the new city. Lysimachus was defeated and slain by Seleucus I in 281 B.C.

Seleucus I gave the kingdom to his son, Antiochus I, who then
ruled over Ephesus. In 190 B.C., Seleucid King Antiochus III, (the
Great), was defeated by the Romans, and the cities of Asia Minor fell
under the dominion of Rome.

During the New Testament period that you are now in, the
city has reached its golden age and become the leading city of Asia
Minor. Ephesus is the main entry point to the Roman provinces, and
it is a great seaport town of many thousands of people. When Roman
rulers visit in Asia Minor, the first port of call is always the city of
Ephesus. The city is built on the Cayster River which provides many
benefits and also some serious problems. During the rainy season of
the springtime, the river floods and silts up the very narrow harbor
leading into Ephesus from the Aegean Sea. Ephesus is a powerful,
wealthy city with many beautiful buildings; however, our greatest
attraction is the temple of Artemis. Another site of considerable note
is the grand theater which we have already visited.

PASTOR: Thank you, Mayor Jason, for this tour.
Several hundred years after the New Testament period, this city will
lose its fight with the river, the harbor will be permanently silted up,
and a grain field will stand in its place. In our day, the city of Ephesus
lies four to five miles from the Aegean Sea. From Ephesus, John, as
the leader of the seven churches, could very easily visit the other cities in the province. It was one of the first cities to practice Caesar
worship with the largest statue of Caesar Domitian erected in its city
square, a statue some sixteen feet tall. In this cosmopolitan setting
John directed his letter to the church at Ephesus.

Let us now meet the pastor of the church at Ephesus. We will
stop here at a small home where the church is meeting. I would like

for you visitors from the twentieth century to meet Timothy, pastor at Ephesus.

TIMOTHY: Welcome to our city and church. Most of our members are slaves or ex-slaves. Today, I am reading a letter to the church from John, who is in prison on the Isle of Patmos. The message has seven points to coincide with the lighting of the seven lamps of a menorah that John saw in a vision. The seven points of the letter are:

1. Words of greeting
2. Words from the Son of Man
3. Words of praise
4. Words of weakness
5. Words of warning
6. Words of reward
7. Words of music

*(Place a seven-branched candlestick by the pulpit and light the seven candles in sequence to the reading)*

The Seven Lamps of Ephesus

1. Greeting *(light candle one)*

"To the angel of the church in Ephesus write:"

2. The Son of Man *(light candle two)*

"The words of him who holds the seven stars in his right hand, who walks among the seven golden lampstands."

3. Praise *(light candle three)*

"I know your works, your toil and your patient endurance, and how you cannot bear evil men but have tested those who call themselves apostles but are not, and found them to be false; I know you are enduring patiently and bearing up for my name's sake, and you have not grown weary. . . . Yet this you have, you hate the work of the Nicolaitans, which I also hate."

4. Weakness *(light candle four)*

"But I have this against you, that you have abandoned the love you had at first."

5. Warning *(light candle five)*

"Remember then from what you have fallen, repent and do the works you did at first. If not, I will come to you and remove your lampstand from its place, unless you repent."

6. Music *(light candle six)*

"He who has an ear, let him hear what the Spirit says to the churches."

7. Reward *(light candle seven)*

"To him who conquers I will grant to eat of the tree of life, which is in the paradise of God."[1]

TIMOTHY: We here at Ephesus are proud of our church's name. Our history goes all the way back to the founding father: Paul. Our church stands in the midst of the seven churches as the Son of man stands in the midst of the seven lampstands. John, the apostle, lived among us here and often traveled out to the other churches to visit and help them. Thus, our city Ephesus was home base for John.

Let me say that our church here is a very strong one. In John's letter to us, as recorded in Revelation, we are praised for our works. This compliment is especially directed to our efforts to root out false teachers: the Nicolaitans. They teach that one can go ahead and worship Caesar and receive his tattoo on the back of the hand or forehead so that one might buy food in the marketplace. They say it is better to compromise and feed one's family than to stand foolishly on principles. They believe the body is of no importance—only the soul is related to God. Thus the worship of Caesar occurs only in the body and will not harm the soul.

I have counseled the church to resist such "watered-down" faith. Our Greek word for "witness" is *martus* —you get your English word *martyr* from it. You might think of testimony as something we stand up and give in church on Wednesday night. For many of you, the word *testimony* has to do with words only. For us, *testimony* means staking our lives on what we believe. Many of our members will be arrested and put to death for their testimonies this week or next week. Yet, I know we will persevere. John has heard of our many martyrs even on the distant Isle of Patmos.

We do have some weaknesses in our church. In rooting out the false teachers, we have lost our brotherly love. John always stressed that love of God is related to our fellow brothers and sisters in Christ. We cannot say we love God and hate our fellow brothers and sisters in Christ. We have lost our original zeal for God and our fellow Christians. It was necessary to rid ourselves of the Nicolaitans and their destructive influence, but in the process, we all have been harmed. We here at Ephesus will have to work at reclaiming our first love. The job will not be easy.

John's letter also contains a warning to us. He calls upon us to repent. We must do a complete about-face and regain our former zeal. The warning declares that if we do not repent, our lampstand will be removed. We in Ephesus know that our city has moved three times in its history. Our city fathers were always looking for higher ground to get away from the marshy ground and the mosquitos. We know the toil and pain of moving. Thus, John's warning is a real one to us. The church that has no message cannot expect to survive.

"He who has an ear, let him hear"—these are words of a hymn we often sing in our church. The words of the hymn call for obedience to the Word of God. We must be more than hearers of the Word. We must be actively involved in doing "the word." There is much work here to be done in Ephesus. Please pray for us that we might endeavor to do it all.

The reward offered to our church in John's letter is quite significant. We are told that we will participate in the "tree of life" "in the paradise of God." At the end of John's "Revelation," we read of a new garden of Eden with the tree of life no longer forbidden but available to all. We will dwell with God and have eternal fellowship with Him. Those words bring hope into the hearts of my people who are being so cruelly persecuted by the Romans.

I know it is time for you to return to the twentieth century. I hope your visit to ancient Ephesus has been a helpful one. Remember our church and the difficulties which are before us. Pray that we will give our testimony even unto death.

PASTOR: Well, let us get back in our time capsule and journey back to the twentieth century. Ah, we have arrived. I hope that our journey to first-century Ephesus has been helpful to you. We have seen that the believing community at Ephesus was brought together through the cross of Christ. In its shadow, they struggled together, were persecuted together, and died together! In that kind of atmosphere, links were established between believers which allowed them to laugh together and cry together.

In our modern church, we miss this serious tone in the word *fellowship.* For most of us "fellowship" is coffee and doughnuts after Sunday School. True fellowship has its abode in the heart. The spiritual cement of this fellowship is the grace of God. Every Christian, no matter where he or she is, has in common with every other Christian the experience of God's grace in the bestowal of salvation. This grace was given by the suffering of Christ on the cross. Thus, in the New Testament church, suffering together was a very essential part of fellowship. Death, imprisonment, and torture were very real possibilities facing Christians. When one Christian experienced it, all felt it through the interlocking network of fellowship.

Here in America, it is safe to be a Christian. We say we can do more by living than by dying. Fellowship has lost some of the dimension of suffering together and even preparing to die together that characterized the Ephesian church. If we Christians are willing to view life as John and the Ephesian Christians did, life and death can have meaning. Either one can be a testimony for the Lord. The important thing is that we not be ashamed of our witness. Rather, we should allow Christ to speak boldly through us. Thus, instead of fearing death, you can see it as a unique opportunity to witness for your faith. Even when martyrdom is no longer a real possibility in our country, your witness should take on life and death overtones. Your Christian witness is something you should stake your life on.

A student in Germany told of his experience when traveling

behind the iron curtain to East Berlin. On Sunday, he looked for a Baptist church in which to worship. He finally found one in a broken-down storefront building. Most of the small congregation was made up of old women and small children. The young pastor gave a very good sermon, but near the end, a look of fear came into his eyes as he glanced at the back door of the church. A young Russian lieutenant had entered the church. Most of the people thought he had come to spy them out.

The pastor hurriedly gave the benediction, and everyone stood to hurry out. Then the young Russian began to speak. He told us that he also was a Baptist. This was the first Sunday of his being away from home. He had promised his parents and home congregation that he would seek out a Baptist church in Berlin. There was hardly a dry eye in the whole church. Afterwards, they all filed by and shook his hand. The student went back to West Germany to the university. The next week, the student received a letter from the pastor of the church in Berlin. The pastor related that some comrades of the young Russian had reported him for attending worship at the Baptist church. As a result, the soldier had been sent to a camp in Siberia.

This young Russian, like the Ephesians, came to know the true meaning of "witness." May we come to know it also!

### Note

1. Some of the material in this chapter is adapted from James L. Blevins, *Revelation as Drama* (Nashville: Broadman Press, 1984), 26-31.

# 13

# John: Rediscovering a Lost Book

*(In this role play, one would switch over to the character of John in the middle of the sermon—using the power of imagination.)*

A great tragedy has occurred in the church! We have lost one of the books of the Bible! Instead of sixty-six, we now have sixty-five. For all practical purposes, we have lost the last book of the Bible: the Book of Revelation. Now, before you start turning in your Bibles to assure yourself that the book is still there, let me go on to say that we have "lost" the book because we are failing to *use* the book.

There are several reasons why Revelation has become the closed book of the Bible. Many of us fear it, or do not understand it. When you were a youngster in Sunday School, perhaps you decided to read the Bible through. You made it through Leviticus, even Deuteronomy, but you could not quite come to grips with the seven-headed creatures and weird monsters in the Book of Revelation. After such an experience, many close their Bibles and wait many years before returning to this last book. Many long for a better understanding of the *last* book of the Bible. Sometimes Bible students are well into seminary before they finally come to grips with Revelation. A student related that he enrolled in An Introduction to the New Testament in College, and, lo and behold, a few weeks before the end of the semester, the professor said, "Now students, we have run out of time, and we won't get to Revelation this semester." Later the student enrolled in a course on Revelation and there encountered the positive message of this last book in our Bible.

Another reason Revelation is a lost book in our Christian Bible is that quite often there is very little information available to the average Christian. The International Sunday School Lessons very seldom come from Revelation, and if they do, they are usually on the seven churches. In my memory, I cannot think of a time when a major denominational Bible study focused on Revelation. In many evangelical churches, there is silence even from the pulpit when it comes to the last book in the Bible. Yet many of you, I am sure, are yearning to know more about this "closed" book.

Perhaps another more important reason for our avoiding the last book of the Bible is that there are so many different kinds of interpretation—there are those who take the predictive approach to Revelation: this last book in the Bible will reveal all the future in detail. They work out Revelation on charts and graphs for almost every moment of the day until the end of the world. Books flood the market carrying that kind of approach. Sometimes extremists in this field would have everything so plotted out that if God wanted to change His mind, He could not because they already have it on their charts! The other extreme approach of interpretation is that everything in Revelation has been fulfilled, and it's just a dull, dead, dry history book. Why read it? Then in between we have all other kinds of interpretation.

Let us not allow this controversy to become a stumbling block, for there is such an important message in the last book of the Bible. Probably the biggest stumbling block in our way is the old millennium question. Many pastors will not preach from the book because of that. Only three verses in Revelation even mention the thousand year reign or millennium. Yet, for so long this has been the major point of contention, and people will ask, "Are you premillennialist, post-, or a-?" I know one theological student who went into examinations for his ordination, and one dear brother on the committee asked him, "Now, young man, which school do you belong to? Are you pre-, post- or a-?" Well, the student knew he was in for it! So he turned around and said, "I'm panmillennialist." The preachers were taken aback. This is a new school, they said, What is it? "Well, it's all going to *pan* out in the end, anyway," the student said. That might well be the "best approach," if we are going to get hung up on the millennium question.

I think it is time we allow the other verses to speak to us and not let the millennium question to hold us back. The book has such a positive message for our day. There are many other excuses or reasons for not studying the last book of the Bible, but I think it is time to put all these aside, for when you have the Alpha, you also need the Omega. When you read the first chapters of the book, you need the last chapter to bring it all together. Open up your Bible to Revelation: if it has been a closed book for you, begin to read it. To help you in studying the book, I will give you a few directions.

First, put it against the time in which it was written. The year is A.D. 95. The Roman Caesars had come to the conclusion that they were divine, particularly Caesar Domitian. He passed a law that statues of himself should be constructed and placed in all cities of Asia Minor. People would be required to fall down and worship the statues three times a day and say: "Caesar is lord!" A tattoo of Caesar's face would be stamped on the back of their hands, or on their foreheads, and this would allow them to buy food in the marketplace. If one refused to worship Caesar, one could be tortured, imprisoned, or even killed. Put yourself in the place of a Christian in that time. The main confession of the early church was: Jesus is Lord! Now they were to bow before Caesar's statue and say that Caesar is lord! John and the twelve disciples at Ephesus led the believers there in not bowing down and worshiping Caesar, and many of the Christians were persecuted or tortured. John, himself, was arrested and sent to a prison island forty miles off the coast of Ephesus called Patmos. There he had to quarry rock in the hot sun and live in a cold, damp cave at night. To help us understand why John wrote Revelation, we have him here as our guest this morning. John, we are happy to have you with us today!

**John:** It's a real joy to be with you folks. I made this long trip to tell you something about a wonderful book in your Bible. Over several months during the time I was in prison on the island of Patmos, I began to receive glorious revelations from God, and God gave me a message to give those Christians in the seven churches—a great message of victory and hope—and my heart glowed within me as I began to write down these marvelous words.

I was faced with a real difficulty. How was I going to get this message back to those Christians who needed to hear? I decided to write my book in *code language*, or symbols, and I think that may be why it is difficult for many of you today. I chose a code that the Jewish people had used down through days of persecution and difficulty—an apocalyptic code.

There are *three* basic codes in my Book of Revelation. First of all, as you read, every *number* has a meaning: seven is a holy number; six stands for imperfection; five is the number of penalty; ten stands for completeness; twelve (a very important number) stands for wholeness. When you come to a large number, underline it and break it down to its basic number. For example, 144,000, one of the key numbers in Revelation, is based on twelve, the complete number of God—the complete people of God.

The second code is also very important. Every *color* has a meaning. Black symbolizes famine; red, warfare; gold, worth or value; and white, conquering or purity. Pale green represents death and dark green: life. Bronze stands for strength. In chapter 1, I preach a whole sermon in color code. I could not openly speak of Christ, so I described Him in color code: white hair of conquering, bronze feet of strength, and His golden girdle of worth. Colors have meanings.

Now the third code is the most important code. Throughout my book, I allow *animals* to represent people. Put yourself in my place: I was in prison, and I wanted to write about Caesar being a very cruel and horrible king. I couldn't come out and say Caesar Domitian is a terrible person. He is a very cruel and ugly man. But I could put in a seven-headed beast to represent him and say all kinds of things about that beast! When I wanted to talk about Christ, I couldn't openly refer to Him as the Savior of the world, so I have a lamb to represent Him. The meanest, vilest animal is the frog: it symbolizes evil. In Revelation 16:13, three frogs appear before the battle of Armageddon. The eagle always brings bad news. Its call echoes some twelve times across the pages of the book. The Greeks used to mimic the sounds of birds or animals. In Greek, the eagle calls out *Quai, quai.* If one says it quickly in Greek, one gets the sound of an eagle. The English translate it *woe.* Some animals just represent qualities, such as the lion: courage and conviction. As you read Revelation and come across one of those animals that you just can't understand, ask yourself a question: Who is the animal representing?

The last thing I'd like to share with you is that in Ephesus, where I served for twenty-five years, there was a large theater where great Greek dramas were held. As I received my revelation from God there on Patmos, I was led of the Spirit to write Revelation as drama. One cannot put a visionary experience into phrase. In Ephesus was a large Greek theater holding some 24,000 people. The stage building was quite unique—it had seven windows for the stage scenery. All the Greek dramas were thus produced in sevens. I also divided my book into seven acts with seven scenes in each act.

**Pastor:** Thank you, John, you've been very helpful. I think these will be good guidelines as we read your book in the Bible. I have a great dream of one day going to Ephesus and taking a group to dramatize the Book of Revelation on the stage. Wouldn't it be glorious to see the great hand of God at work in a great drama in which people could visualize the message of Christ to John?

In Revelation, you see the sweep of human history—and the hand of God in that history. Act I begins with seven large golden lampstands in a semicircle around the stage. Each lampstand represents one of the seven churches in Asia Minor. The stage is dark. Suddenly the first lampstand is lighted. Just imagine a painting of Ephesus in the first window of the stage, and a voice offstage begins to read the

letter to the church: "To the angel of the church in Ephesus write . . ."
As each lampstand is lighted, one of the seven letters is read aloud. In
the middle of the seven churches stands the Son of man dressed in
the white robes of a great priest. Quickly, Act II comes on the stage,
and we have the act of the seven seals. A lamb walks out on the stage,
and He holds a scroll with seven golden seals on it, and as each seal is
broken, action takes place on the stage. We see the kind of world
Christians will have to live in down through history. The four horses
of the apocalypse appear: the conqueror, warfare, famine, and death.
Persecution stalks the martyrs. And yet, that wonderful positive
message prevails: God has you in His hands. You are under His seal of
protection.

Act III dawns before us, and seven angels enter with seven trumpets. As each trumpet is blown, one-third of the world is destroyed,
and it is an act of warning to the wicked—repent, before it is too late.
Destruction comes by natural calamities, by warfare, and by other
means of God's design. Act IV is probably the most important act
because it shows the beginning struggle between good and evil
through seven short pageants. It begins with the birth of Christ, and
we encounter Satan and his two helpers described as horrible-looking
beasts. We see the conflict down through human history until, suddenly, that conflict will end in one large battle between good and evil
at the end of the world. Act V opens when the seven angels come
back out, bearing great bowls of wrath, and this represents the final
judgment of God upon the earth. These plagues are very similar to
those in Exodus. These plagues come upon the face of the earth—a
last act of God's judgment. In Act VI, the judgment of God is carried
forth on the earth in seven scenes. Rome is destroyed, and three
chapters describe it in great detail. Suddenly Christ returns, and the
last battle takes place. Those events open the door to the marvelous
act of all acts: Act VII. New Jerusalem comes down from heaven, God
is in our midst, and Revelation ends on a glorious note: God has made
the world right, and He dwells with it again! Why deny ourselves
that great message of victorious hope!

I am afraid I see developing a "losing team" kind of psychology in Christians today. We are so very similar to those seven churches in Revelation. I am sure that if you interviewed some of those early Christians they would have said, "Caesar is going to win out; Christianity isn't strong enough." They might have developed a "losing team" psychology. And yet I would have loved to have been there when the little church was meeting in the cave, and the pastor stood and said, "Brethren, we have received a letter from John, all the way from the Isle of Patmos." As he began to read the Book of Revelation, one could see smiles creeping across the faces of those young Christians: there is hope—we *are* on a winning team!

I remember in my senior year of high school our football team had a losing team. Now, that is terrible! The news spread all across our town. You would walk to the business area, and it looked as if a dark cloud had just settled over. Everybody was mourning for the high-school football team. You would come to the church on Sunday morning, and even the pastor would come out with a frown. It was a bad year!—a losing year! I am so grateful for the Book of Revelation and the fact that it is in our Bible. If there is any one sentence that would sum up the whole book, it would be: *God is reigning!* As the old Negro spiritual says, "He's got the whole world in His hands." Communism is not going to dictate the final end of our world society. There is no philosophy that will show us the future of the world. Revelation says God has brought us into being: God will bring us to an end. Hitler boasted about ruling for a thousand years, and he barely made it through ten. Persons throughout the ages have been just like Caesar Domitian, declaring all the great monuments they were going to build, the dreams they were going to fulfill. God does it in Revelation: "I am in control of things," He says.

This should give us a whole different perspective toward the work of the church. If we are on the winning team, we should have joy on our faces. We have the victory already. It took a lot of courage for John, sitting in a Roman prison, to write that God is going to rule. It took a lot of courage for John to stand and say, "The Romans are going to fall"—even years before it happened. John had that message of victory in his heart. I'm happy to be on a winning team. I think we need to broadcast that good news to the world and share this message of victorious joy with all people! A losing team is one in which everyone sits back and watches other people do the work. If we are on the winning team, we need to get out there on the playing field and play ball! Get involved in this great message that Christ has given to us.

I taught on the college level for seven years, so many young people would come into my office from Baptist families, and they would yearn and long for a Christianity that was dynamic—one that would offer them a challenge. I knew that many of them had to have the highest kind of grades just to get into college; many of them competed on the football field, and they had to have the strongest bodies. Just in the last Olympics, we saw record after record being broken. A great challenge is being placed before the youth today, but so often they come into the church and find no challenge whatsoever. They view Christianity, as is, cold and dead. Over and over, I would point out to these young people verses in the New Testament in which Jesus says: if you will follow Me, take up your cross! That's the greatest challenge in the world!

The call goes forth for people to be proud of what they are. We are on the winning team. Jesus Christ is King of kings and Lord of lords! That is something to cheer about—an exciting dynamic message to be shared. It should be a privilege for us to go through the doors of the sanctuary this morning and say to the people: "God reigns! Jesus Christ is the victorious King, and you can know this triumphant joy in your life."

Well, I've made my case. I want to put Revelation back in the Bible. In this year, I think we need to hear it: a positive message of triumphant hope for these days!

# Appendix: Resources

***General Resources***

The Three Faces of Drama in the Church: Drama

Staging a Musical Drama

The Dramatic Monologue

To order these videotapes, write BTN, 127 Ninth Avenue, North, Nashville, Tennessee 37234

Bausch, William J. *Story Telling: Faith and Imagination.* Mystic, Connecticut: Twenty-third Publications, 1984.

Blevins, James L. *Revelation as Drama.* Nashville: Broadman Press, 1983.

Brown, David M. *Dramatic Narrative in Preaching.* Valley Forge: Judson Press, 1981.

Freeman, Harold. *Variety in Biblical Preaching.* Waco, Texas: Word Books, 1987.

Hubbard, David Allan. *Strange Heroes.* Philadelphia and New York: A. J. Holman Company, 1971.

Ivins, Dan. *God's People in Transition.* Nashville, Tennessee: Broadman Press, 1981.

*Monologues for Church.* Nashville: Convention Press, 1982.

Wiesel, Elie. *Messengers of God.* New York: Random Books, 1976.

Everett Robertson. *Introduction to Church Drama.* Nashville: Convention Press, 1978. (Suggestions for costumes and makeup)

### Acting

Armstrong, Chloe. *Oral Interpretation of Biblical Literature.* Minneapolis: Burgess Publishing Co., 1968.

Lessac, Arthur. *The Use and Training of the Human Voice.* New York: Drama Book Specialists, Inc., 1967.

McGraw, Charles. *Acting Is Believing.* New York: Holt, Rinehart and Winston, 1965.

Shepard, Richmond, *Mime: The Technique of Silence.* New York: Drama Book Specialists, Inc., 1971.

Spolin, Viola. *Improvisation for the Theater.* Evanston: Northwestern University Press, 1970.

### Costume

Barton, Lucy. *Appreciating Costume.* Boston: W. H. Baker, 1969.

Barton, Lucy. *Historical Costume for the State.* Boston: W. H. Baker, 1961.

Barton, Lucy, *Costuming the Biblical Play.* Boston: W. H. Baker.

Fernald, Mary. *Costume Design and Making: A Practical Handbook.* New York: Theatre Arts Books, 1967.

### Makeup

Corson, Richard. *Stage Makeup.* New York: Appleton-Century-Crofts, 1960.

Cummings, Richard. *One Hundred and One Masks.* New York: David McKay Co., 1968.

Knapp, Jack Stuart. *The Technique of Stage Makeup.* Boston: W. H. Baker.

### Makeup and Costume Supplies

ABC Theatrical Rentals, 536 West Washington, Phoenix, Arizona 85003

Atlanta Costume Company, 2409 Piedmont Road, N.E., Atlanta, Georgia 30324

Texas Scenic Company, 5423 Jackwood Drive, San Antonio, Texas 78228

Theatre House, Inc., P. O. Box 2090, Covington, Kentucky 41012-2090